Unfinished Dreams

Unfinished Dreams
Contemporary Poetry of Acadie

FRED COGSWELL & JO-ANNE ELDER
Translators and Editors

with an Introduction by
RAOUL BOUDREAU

Goose Lane Editions

Published with the assistance of the Canada Council and the New Brunswick Department of Tourism, Recreation and Heritage, 1990.

Cover art: "Deux oiseaux survolant un paysage" by Paul Édouard Bourque
Book design by Julie Scriver
Printed in Canada by Hignell Printing

Canadian Cataloguing in Publication Data

Main entry under title:

Unfinished dreams: contemporary poetry of Acadie

Includes bibliographical references and index.
ISBN 0-86492-132-2

1. Canadian poetry (French) — Acadian authors — Translations into English.
2. Canadian poetry (French) — 20th century — Translations into English.
3. Canadian poetry (English) — Translations from French.
I. Cogswell, Fred, 1917- . II. Elder, Jo-Anne.

PS8295.5.M37U63 1990   C841'.5408.09715   C90-097693-4
PQ3914.5E5U63 1990

Goose Lane Editions
248 Brunswick Street
Fredericton, New Brunswick
Canada E3B 1G9

CONTENTS

ACKNOWLEDGEMENTS

GUY ARSENAULT "To Celebrate September," "Backyard Tableau" and "The Wharf" were originally published as "Célébrer septembre," "Tableau de back yard," and "Le Quai" in *Acadie Rock* © Guy Arsenault, 1973. Used by permission of Les Éditions d'Acadie. Earlier versions of the translations of "To Celebrate September" and "The Wharf" were published in *Canadian Literature*, No. 68-69 © Fred Cogswell, 1976. "Writer's Block" was originally published as "Rien d'écrit" in *La poésie acadienne, 1948-1988* (Les Écrits des Forges & Le Castor Astral, 1988) © Guy Arsenault. Used by permission of the author. "Women" and "We Can't" were originally published as "des femmes . . . " and "on ne peut pas . . . " in *Y'a toutes sortes de personnes* © Guy Arsenault, 1989. Used by permission of Michel Henry Éditeur.

GEORGES BOURGEOIS "Myself with a Sharp Knife," "Poem in Monochrome" and "Ode to the Mackerel Fishers" were originally published as "Moi, avec un couteau tranchant . . . ," "Poème en camaïeu (senteur de gros frette)" and "Ode aux d'riveux de maquereaux" in *Les Îles Fidgi dans la baie de Cocagne* © Georges Bourgeois, 1986. Used by permission of Les Éditions Perce-Neige.

HUGUETTE BOURGEOIS "Mutilations" and "Dogs, Men and Women" were originally published as "Mutilations" and "Les chiens errent . . . " in *Les Rumeurs de l'amour* © Huguette Bourgeois, 1984. Used by permission of Les Éditions Perce-Neige. "Landscape," "If," "Here in this Room," "Adieu" and "Rain-Refrain" were originally published as "Paysage," "Si," "ici dans cette chambre . . . ," "Adieu" and "Refrain de pluie" in *L'Enfant-fleur* © Huguette Bourgeois, 1988. Used by permission of Les Éditions d'Acadie.

HERMÉNÉGILDE CHIASSON "Between the Season of Extravagant Love and the Season of Raspberries," "So That You Can't Fly Away," "All the King's Horses," "Eugénie Melanson," "Blue" and "Red" were originally published as "Entre la saison du fol amour et la saison des framboises," "Pour pas que tu t'envoles," "Tous les chevaux du roi," "Eugénie Melanson," "Bleu" and "Rouge" in *Mourir à Scoudouc* © Herménégilde Chiasson, 1974. Used by permission of Les Éditions d'Acadie. Earlier versions of the translations of "Between the Season of Extravagant Love and the Season of Raspberries" and "All the King's Horses" were published in *Canadian Literature*, No. 68-69 © Fred Cogswell, 1976. "Plain," "(sic)" and "Constellation" were were originally published as "Plaine," "(sic)" and "Constellation" in *Prophéties* © Herménégilde Chiasson, 1986. Used by permission of Michel Henry Éditeur.

ANNE CLOUTIER "Detour and return IN THE TROPICS," "Picture Us There" and "In a Room . . . " were originally published as "détour et retour DANS LES TROPIQUES," "l'intensité d'un doute . . . " and "Dans une chambre . . . "

in *Éloizes*, No. 9 © Anne Cloutier, 1984. Used by permission of the author.

CLARENCE COMEAU "Beside your Lovely Fields . . ." and "Cries of Love and Silence" were originally published as "A côté de tes beaux champs de trèfles . . ." and "Cris d'amour et de silence" in *Entre amours et silences* © Clarence Comeau, 1980. Used by permission of Les Éditions d'Acadie.

LOUIS COMEAU "As if for change . . . ," "Fear" and "To my Father" were originally published as "Comme pour changer," "La peur" and "À mon père" in *Moosejaw* © Louis Comeau, 1981. Used by permission of Les Éditions Perce-Neige.

FRANCE DAIGLE "And it went on" was originally published as "Et cela dura" in *Éloizes*, No. 11 © France Daigle, 1985. "Mediterranean Women (1-2)" was originally published as "Méditerranéennes (1-2)" in *Éloizes, no. 7, 1988* © France Daigle. "Mediterranean Women (1-4)" was originally published as "Méditerranéennes (1-4)" in *La Poésie acadienne, 1948-1988* (Les Écrits des Forges & Le Castor Astral, 1988) © France Daigle. Both poems used by permission of the author.

RONALD DESPRÉS "Hymn to Spring" was originally published as "Hymne au printemps" in *Le Balcon des dieux inachevés* (Les Éditions Garneau, 1969) © Ronald Després. Used by permission of the author. An earlier version of this translation was published in *A Second Hundred Poems of Modern Québec* (Fiddlehead Poetry Books, 1971) and *Canadian Literature*, No. 68-69, 1976 © Fred Cogswell. "My Acadie," "Poetry Night in Acadie," "I Thought of You All Day," "I Loved You," "Suddenly it was Good to be Alive," "Hands" and "Your Footsteps" were originally published as "Mon Acadie," "Nuit de la poésie acadienne," "J'ai pensé à toi toute la journée," "Je t'ai aimée," "Tout à coup, il faisait bon vivre," "Les Mains," and "Tes pas" in *Paysages en contrebande . . . à la frontière du songe* © Ronald Després, 1974. Used by permission of Les Éditions d'Acadie. Earlier versions of the translations of "I Loved You" and "I Thought of You All Day" were published in *A Second Hundred Poems of Modern Québec* (Fiddlehead Poetry Books, 1971) and *Canadian Literature*, No. 68-69, 1976 © Fred Cogswell. An earlier version of the translation of "Hands" was published in *A Second Hundred Poems of Modern Québec* (Fiddlehead Poetry Books, 1971) © Fred Cogswell.

ROSE DESPRÉS "Hymn to Light" was originally published as "Cantique à la lumiére" in *Fièvre de nos mains* © Rose Després, 1982. Used by permission of Les Éditions Perce-Neige. "At the Star-port" was originally published as "Au port astral" in *Requiem en saule pleureur* © Rose Després, 1986. Used by permission of Les Éditions d'Acadie. "Excerpts from a Poem Sequence" was originally published in *La Poésie acadienne, 1948-1988* (Les Écrits des Forges & Le Castor Astral, 1988) © Rose Després. Used by permission of the author.

DANIEL DUGAS "Michelin," "The Red Scarf" and "In the Star-heap over our Heads" were originally published as "Michelin," "Le Foulard rouge" and

"Dans le tas d'étoiles au-dessus de nos têtes" in *L'Hara-Kiri de Santa-Gougouna* © Daniel Dugas, 1983. Used by permission of Les Éditions Perce-Neige.

CALIXTE DUGUAY "To Marie," "To Have a Homeland" and "The Stigmata of Silence" were originally published as "À Marie" "Avoir un pays" and "Les Stigmates du silence" in *Les Stigmates du silence* © Calixte Duguay, 1975. Used by permission of Les Éditions d'Acadie.

GÉRARD ÉTIENNE "Ah My Love Flutters . . . " was originally published as "Ah voltige mon amour . . . " in *La Raison et mon amour* (Les Éditions Port-au-princiennes, 1961) © Gérard Étienne. "It is snowing outside . . ." was originally published as "Il neige dehors . . . " in *La Poésie acadienne, 1948-1988* (Les Écrits des Forges & Le Castor Astral, 1988) © Gérard Étienne. Both poems used by permission of the author.

LÉONARD FOREST "Former Seasons" and "And I Dreamed of a Great Black Sun" were originally published as "Saisons antérieures" and "et j'ai rêvé d'un grand soleil noir" in *Saisons antérieures* © Léonard Forest, 1973. An earlier version of the translation of "And I Dreamed of a Great Black Sun" was published in *Canadian Literature*, No. 68-69 © Fred Cogswell, 1976. "My Royal Roads" and "Itineraries" were originally published as "Mes Chemins du roi" and "Itinéraires" in *Comme en Florence* © Léonard Forest, 1979. All poems used by permission of Les Éditions d'Acadie.

MELVIN GALLANT "Extracts from *An Island Summer*" were originally published in *L'Été insulaire* © Melvin Gallant, 1982. Used by permission of Les Éditions d'Acadie.

ULYSSE LANDRY "And this Program . . . " and "Screaming Against Tomorrow's Silence" were originally published as "Et ce programme . . . " and "Crier à tue-tête contre le silence de demain" in *Tabous aux épines de sang* © Ulysse Landry, 1977. Used by permission of Les Éditions d'Acadie.

JEANNINE LANDRY-THÉRIAULT "Femmenolence" and "Earlier Seasons" were originally published as "Femmenolence" and "Saisons antérieures" in *Éloizes*, vol. 7, no. 1 © Jeannine Landry-Thériault, 1986. Used by permission of the author.

GÉRALD LEBLANC "Architect of the Feast" was originally published as "Architecte de la fête" in *Géographie de la nuit rouge* © Gérald Leblanc, 1984. Used by permission of Les Éditions d'Acadie. "First place" and "Complicity" were originally published as "premier lieu" and "connivence" in *Lieux transitoires* © Gérald Leblanc, 1986. Used by permission of Michel Henry Éditeur. "Acadielove," "To Love You," "January Stillness" and "Voices" were originally published as "acadie-love," "pour t'aimer," "le silence de janvier" and "voix" in *L'Extrême frontière* © Gérald Leblanc, 1988. Used by permission of Les Éditions d'Acadie.

MONIQUE LEBLANC "End of the Film" and "Park Portugal, Far from the

Mainland" were originally published as "La Fin du film" and "Parc Portugal, loin du continent" in *La Poésie acadienne, 1948-1988* (Les Écrits des Forges & Le Castor Astral, 1988) © Monique Leblanc. Used by permission of the author.

RAYMOND GUY LEBLANC "Flower," "Winter," "Land-cry," "Plan for a Country (Acadie-Québec)," and "I am Acadian" were originally published as "Fleur," "Hiver," "Cri de terre," "Projet de pays (Acadie-Québec)" and "Je suis Acadien" in *Cri de terre* © Raymond Leblanc, 1972. Used by permission of Les Éditions d'Acadie. Earlier versions of the translations of "Winter" and "Land-cry" were published in *Canadian Literature*, No. 68-69 © Fred Cogswell, 1976. "Poem, July 1982," "Poem for Lise," "With Her," "Past Midnight," "Time Turns to Tenderness," "Birth" and "The Trigram of the Unfathomable Heart" were originally published as "Poème du mois de juillet 1982," "Poème pour Lise," "Avec elle," "Passé minuit," "Le Temps tourne à la tendresse," "Naissance" and "Le Trigramme du coeur insondable" in *Chants d'amour et d'espoir* © Raymond Guy Leblanc, 1989. Used by permission of Michel Henry Éditeur.

HUGUETTE LÉGARÉ "The Coffee Cup" and "Sinister Ritual" were originally published as "La Tasse de café" and "Rituel sinistre" in *Le Ciel végétal* (La pensée universelle, 1976) © Huguette Légaré. Used by permission of the author. "Pollen tempest" was originally published as "La Tempête du pollen" in *La Tempête du pollen* © Huguette Légaré, 1978. Used by permission of Les Éditions Saint-Germain-des-Prés. "The Moon" was originally published as "La Lune" in *L'Amarinée* © Huguette Légaré, 1979. Used by permission of Les Éditions Saint-Germain-des-Prés. "Beside the Hotel" was originally published as "À côté de l'hôtel" in *Brun marine* © Huguette Légaré, 1981. Used by permission of Les Éditions d'Acadie.

DYANE LÉGER "The Hangar of the Haunted" was orginally published as "Le Hangar des hantés" in *Graines de fées* © Dyane Léger, 1980. "Latent Lesbians" was originally published as "Lesbiennes latentes" in *Sorcière de vent* © Dyane Léger, 1983. Both poems used by permission of Les Éditions d'Acadie.

HENRI-DOMINIQUE PARATTE "Blood Red" was originally published as "Rouge Sang" in *Éloizes*, No. 9 © Henri-Dominique Paratte, 1984. "I Read Poetry . . ." was originally published as "Je lis la poésie . . . " in *Éloizes*, No. 11 © Henri-Dominique Paratte, 1985. Both poems used by permission of the author.

ROBERT PICHETTE "Miscou" and "Imaginings" were originally published as "Miscou" and "Chimères" in *Chimères, poèmes d'amour et d'eau claire* © Robert Pichette, 1982. "Ancient Tapestry" was originally published as "Tapisserie ancienne" in *Bellérophon* © Robert Pichette, 1987. All poems used by permission of Les Éditions d'Acadie.

MARTIN PITRE "Dark and Light" and "A Wrinkled Rough Copy" were originally published as "Noir sur jour" and "un brouillon ridé" in *À s'en mordre les dents* © Martin Pitre, 1982. Used by permission of Les Éditions Perce-Neige. "In fact . . . " was originally published as "En fait . . ." in *Éloizes*, vol. 7, no. 2 © Martin Pitre, 1986. Used by permission of the author.

MAURICE RAYMOND "The Evidence and the Miracle," "Simply to Believe . . . ," "The Limits of Speech," "Unstable Passers-by," "Builders of the Void" and "The Wind" were originally published as "Les Évidences et la merveille," "Simplement croire," "Les Limites de la parole," "Les Passants débiles," "Les Constructeurs du vide" and "Le Vent" in *Implorable désert* © Maurice Raymond, 1988. Used by permission of Les Éditions d'Acadie.

RINO MORIN ROSSIGNOL "It was love . . . " was originally published as "C'était l'amour . . . " in *Éloizes*, vol. 9 © Rino Morin Rossignol, 1984. Used by permission of the author. "Baobab" was originally published in *Les boas ne touchent pas aux lettres d'amour* © Rino Morin Rossignol, 1988. Used by permission of Les Éditions Perce-Neige.

ALBERT ROY "Rage," "Carving" and "Marthe la 'waitresse'" were originally published as "Rage," "Sculpture" and "Marthe la 'waitresse'" in *Foullis d'un brayon* © Albert Roy, 1980. Used by permission of Les Éditions d'Acadie.

ROSEANN RUNTE "Chillote Song," "Easter Island" and "From Pubnico to Sainte-Anne-du-Ruisseau" were originally published as "Chanson chillote," "Isla de Pascua" and "De Pubnico à Sainte-Anne-du-Ruisseau" in *Éloizes*, vol. 7, no. 1 © Roseann Runte, 1986. All poems used by permission of the author.

ROMÉO SAVOIE "Peeping Eurydice" was originally published as "Eurydice voyeuse" in *Duo de démesure* © Roméo Savoie, 1981. "The Idea of Leaving" and "The Crowd" were originally published as "l'idée de partir" and "la foule" in *Trajets dispersés* © Roméo Savoie, 1989. All poems used with the permission of Les Éditions d'Acadie.

TRANSLATORS' PREFACE

COMPOSING AN ANTHOLOGY of poetry is, to begin with, a dangerous enterprise, loaded with the discomforts of canonization: how does one choose important poems, and when one has finished doing it, what exactly is the end product? At times it seems necessary to sacrifice "quality" (however that may be defined) in order to include works that are representative of some aspect of the culture concerned. Carrying out this task for readers from a different cultural group and familiar with a different literature is an even more humbling, although (we hope) a valuable activity, and translation is probably the riskiest of all exercises. Poems that will be read in one way by readers of the poet's culture are likely to be read differently by those unfamiliar with the literary conventions, influential works and extra-literary forces that have shaped them. These, too, constitute language. Literary translations from outside of Québec are something of an exception, though probably not as much so as the translation of English-Canadian literature into French can be.

A poem itself is either a literal or a free translation from living experience. Despite the difficulties involved, poets — with the aid of Factor X, commonly called the Muse — have often used words, forms and rhythms to reproduce or transcend the experiences that prompted their poems and arouse similar feelings in the reader. According to one view, the translator simply finds equivalent words with sufficient euphony and nuances of feeling in his own language. In other words, the experience of translating is much less arduous than the experience of writing an original poem, and, if the Muse is sufficiently kind, comparable results are quite possible. In the case of translating modern poetry from French into English, a number of the problems found in other language combinations are eliminated. The form of most modern French verse is not strictly metrical but is either cadenced in its rhythms or visual and concerned with presenting an image on a line basis in poetry and a paragraph basis in poetic prose. Moreover, since both French and English developed when Europe was one culture, there were equivalent words with equivalent nuances of feeling established traditionally to cover any meaning and feelings that each culture wished to convey. Despite the rise of nationalism, Acadian and Maritime literature, for instance, have shared some common roots and an evolution that, while distinct, has often been parallel.

Nonetheless, it is difficult to say whether the untranslatable phrase is the exception or the rule. According to a second view, the discovery of a word or a phrase that fits into a number of stylistic systems is a happy coincidence. Translators must choose whether and how to respect semantic precisions, cadence, rhyme, plays on words, intertextual references, phonetic patterns, recurring images, anglicisms, neologisms, ambiguities or whatever other elements mark the work, and determine their place in the textual hierachy. One of the initial decisions for this volume was to place as many of the anglicisms and neologisms as possible in italics, rather than simply retaining them in the translation. In this way, the relations among various cultural and linguistic systems evoked in the poem should be somewhat clearer.

A poem that is particularly strong in some aspect is not necessarily as strong in that way once it is translated — although sometimes, through the same artistic magic that might happen on a blank page, the reverse may be true and the translation may be stronger. Since some poems, by the serendipity of sound, translate more felicitously than others, the editors' choice of poems has been determined by the merit of the translations as poems in their own right. It took the translation of more than five hundred poems to produce this volume.

There cannot really be an equivalent of a text in its completeness and its uniqueness. Nor can translations be read as simple copies. What you will read here are, instead, the results of the largely intuitive processes of writing, modifying and selecting which, we hope, will say as many things as the original, though not necessarily the same things, and poems that can be read as simply and richly as the original poems.

Translation is an experience in which several minds are often better than one. The poems of *Unfinished Dreams* have benefitted by the collaboration of the two editors, the suggestions of Susanne Alexander and Raoul Boudreau, and, in many instances, from those of the authors concerned. It may be noted here that the free and less literal translations in this volume have come about through authorial revision. We thank them for their valuable suggestions in shaping this collection.

We would like to dedicate this anthology to those who have inspired it. Fred Cogswell would like to dedicate his part in creating this book to Marie White (née Girouard), his maternal grandmother, whose goodness and beauty of character formed, at an early age, his concept of womanhood. Jo-Anne Elder's effort was shared, in every poem along the way, with Carlos Gomes, who brought the gift of water and rode the waves under the bridge.

FRED COGSWELL & JO-ANNE ELDER

POETRY AS ACTION

IN ABOUT TWENTY YEARS, Acadian poetry has made remarkable progress. At the beginning of the 1960's, work by Acadian poets was published infrequently, so rarely, in fact, that it was difficult to speak of an Acadian poetry as such. Today, publications appear regularly and with increasing frequency; they demonstrate a recognizable thematic pattern and their continuity is ensured by a group of writers who, while maintaining their individuality, are conscious of shared ideals and collective goals. Thus the oft-repeated question about the existence of an Acadian poetry, or for that matter of an Acadian literature, has finally become a thing of the past.

The best way to measure the progress of Acadian poetry is to take note of its real, if still modest, presence in the francophone world. Although most Europeans continue to assume that Canadian francophones are Québécois, Acadian poetry has itself appeared and been studied in literary journals and at conferences in France and in Belgium, and Acadian poets have read their work, and had it read, in these countries as well as in Switzerland, Africa, and Louisiana. This external recognition, essential to the development of the literature, began, naturally, in Québec, where there are now innumerable commentaries, given both publicly and privately, on and by Acadian poets.

Acadian poetry has therefore made its entrance in distant places around the world. But by a typically Canadian paradox, it is less well known by its anglophone neighbours, just as the poetry of New Brunswick written in English is unfamiliar to most Acadians. Recent history has proven beyond the shadow of a doubt that the concept of the "two solitudes" is still very present. Yet it is only through a better understanding of each other (without, of course, closing our eyes to the real differences among us) that we will be able to develop more neighbourly relations, thereby permitting the optimal development of the two linguistic communities of this province and this country. All those who share this goal — and I am convinced that they are in the majority — will applaud the arrival of this English-language anthology of Acadian poetry.

This anthology focusses on recent Acadian poetry, written during a period sometimes described as the "Acadian Renaissance." It does not include the Acadian poets of the 1950's, whose poetry was religious, patriotic and conformist in both form and content. Proposing a theocentric vision of the world, the poetry of the 50's presented Acadie and Acadians as the chosen people of God who, because of their unfailing attachment to the Catholic faith (in spite of their suffering and misery) served as a pious model for others. Inciting people to prayer and thanksgiving, never to rebellion, the poets of the 50's, Eddy Boudreau, Napoléon Landry and François-Moïse Lanteigne, were later regarded as relics to be rejected rather than models to be emulated by the young poets who, at the end of the 1960's, gave an energetic push to the "Acadian Renaissance."

In the four volumes which he published between 1958 and 1968, Ronald Després acted as a forerunner of this movement, even though his work was quite detached from nationalist themes. Because of his modernism, through which he was able to achieve the simultaneous creation of an image and its linguistic expression, his poetry marked a turning point in Acadian poetry and remains today one of its most successful examples, combining the mastery of verse and rhythm, the accuracy and the range of imagery, the richness and the originality of language. Despite the fact that he was the only poet whose work was published in Acadie in the 60's, Després was warmly received in Québec, where he immediately won a place among "French-Canadian" poets. In the 1970's, when Les Éditions d'Acadie collected his best poems in *Paysages en contrebande . . . à la frontière du songe* (1974), Després re-emerged as an inspiration and example for the young poets, not as a result of the content of his poetry, but because it proved that it was possible to be both an Acadian and a modern poet.

But the work of a single poet cannot itself constitute a national poetry. So the true birth of Acadian poetry must be situated later, at the beginning of the 1970's, when a group of writers sharing common ideals was formed and, through mutual influence, began to ensure regular and frequent publication of their work. This "Acadian Renaissance" was a decisive period not only for the literature of Acadie but for every aspect of its history, when a number of connected factors permitted the crystallization and expression of long-sublimated collective aspirations. Certainly, the wave of Québec nationalism overflowed into Acadie during this period. But it was also a time of intense pride for Acadians because of the election of Louis Robichaud, New Brunswick's first Acadian premier, and the founding of the Université de Moncton, which propelled Acadie out of 19th-century folklore into 20th-century interpretations of Marxism, class struggle, power relations and the resulting student protests. It was also during this period that Antonine Maillet's *La Sagouine* began its pilgrimage around the world, that Québec journals such as *Liberté* and *Écrits du Canada français* devoted special issues to Acadie and to Acadian poetry, that a major survey of poetic activity in Acadie revealed a multitude of previously hidden poets, that Les Éditions d'Acadie was founded and began to publish the work of Acadian writers.

Like the nationalist literature of Québec, the poetry born of this feverish and energetic period was "a cry to fend off death." The urgency of speech, the simple existence of a poetry belonging to Acadie were the most important "messages" of this early work, more important, in fact, than the actual subject matter. Three of the first collections published by Éditions d'Acadie are exemplary of this type of nationalism: *Cri de terre* by Raymond LeBlanc (1972), *Acadie Rock* by Guy Arsenault (1973) and *Mourir à Scoudouc* by Herménégilde Chiasson (1974).

In the strong and clear poems of *Cri de terre*, Raymond LeBlanc denounces, with a combination of introspection and steel-edged words and without a trace of complacency, the unacceptable living conditions of his people:

> I am Acadian
> Which means
> Stuffed dispersed bought alienated sold out
> rebellious. A here there and everywhere
> Man torn open towards the future
> ("I am Acadian," p. 121)

LeBlanc's poetry is also, however, an energetic and formidable movement towards the liberation and the re-affirmation of self:

> A phantom ship I have risen to the river's surface
> Toward the fulness of human tides
> And I have thrown the crowd to the promises of the
>   future
> ("Land-Cry," p. 120)

In *Acadie Rock*, published in 1973 when he was still a high school student, Guy Arsenault revives a fundamental poetic form: using and juxtaposing objects and lists. By naming elements of Acadian culture that contempt and shame had relegated to the backyard of history, he re-appropriates them, transforming "le chiac," the ultimate object of shame, into a treasure — a source of pride. (For this reason, his texts are the most difficult to render faithfully in translation). He thus creates a subversive reversal of perspectives, using discreet humour and mockery:

> mosquito bites
> banana peel
> bottle cap
> pod borer
> *popsicle* stick
> potato bug
> . . . as if everybody knew everybody else
>
> ("Backyard Tableau," p. 30)

Herménégilde Chiasson must be recognized as the third founding poet of modern Acadie. Connecting the real and the unreal, the violence of condemnation and rebellion with the fluid tenderness of a nostalgic dream, Chiasson produces a *tour de force* from which emerges a particular beauty that cradles and shakes us at the same time:

> Acadie, my too beautiful desecrated love, you whom I
> would never take into white sheets, the sheets that
> you have torn in order to make white flags like the
> fields of snow that you have sold like your old fence
> posts, your old barns, your old legends, your old
> dreams . . .
>
> ("Red," p. 48)

LeBlanc, Arsenault and Chiasson influenced Acadian poetry because they were equal to the historical context in which they found themselves; they knew how to belie the prejudicial attitude that poetry committed to a cause is inferior poetry. In fact, quite the opposite seemed to be true: the nationalist movement inspired them, pushing them to peaks of artistic achievement, giving them unforgettable tones: the incisive writing of LeBlanc, the mocking sarcasm of Arsenault, the jazzy pain of Chiasson. For these writers, poetry was not a solitary activity but the incandescence of a fire simmering in an entire class of Acadians, adjusting spontaneously to collective goals and aspirations. Both action and event, their poems became the founding act of a revitalized nation and its literature.

For once, Acadians could take advantage of their exploitation. And, unlike much of contemporary art, their poetic activity did not suffer from traces of illegitimate, individualistic or gratuitous creation. It is perhaps this characteristic which radically distinguishes Acadians from their anglophone contemporaries, whose work tends to be more intro-spective. Having an urgent cause to defend, a culture to save, Acadian writers took up their pen to affirm their very existence. Anything else — whatever was left for others — was only literature. In a recent re-view, Alain Masson makes a clear comment about Acadian poetry in New Brunswick:

> Acadian poetry outlines a unique and autonomous tradition, published in Moncton, poorly known to the French, considered foreign by the Québécois. The same cannot be said, however, of the literature of the province written in the American language.
>
> [. . .] The truth is that there is a cruel dissymetry: on one side, there is New Brunswick, administrative subdivision of a cultural empire of which the capitals are New York and Hollywood; on the other side, there is a small nation whose *survival is threatened by this empire,* but who has learned how to give itself a cultural life all of its own.[1]
>
> (Author's italics)

These different positions explain the mutual lack of understanding between the two literatures.

Nonetheless, Acadian poets of the Renaissance strongly felt the col-lective responsibility connected to their writing, often to such a degree that they sometimes felt paralyzed by it. LeBlanc and Arsenault did not publish new collections for sixteen years, Chiasson for ten. Fortunately, the founding poets had emulators who could ensure the survival of Acadian poetry. With Calixte Duguay, for instance, songs melt into poems with simple, strong images of visceral patriotism, at once full of tenderness and torn apart by the open wounds of alienation:

---

1 Alain Masson, review of *Langues et littératures au Nouveau-Brunswick* (Moncton: Éditions d'Acadie, 1986. English edition: *A Literary and Lin-guistic History of New Brunswick.* Fredericton: Goose Lane Editions, 1985.) in the *Revue de l'Université de Moncton,* vol. 21, no. 1, 1988, pp. 192-3.

> To say, My Acadie
> As they say, My China
> As they will say one day
> Maybe,
> My *Kébec*
> And to feel in your womb
> A quivering
> Like hunger for bread from home
> And the thrill of belonging
> > ("To Have a Homeland," p. 82)

And in the work of Ulysse Landry, pain takes the form of provocation and violence:

> Too often we have mentioned
> the exploits of our fathers
> Too long we have mourned
> the woes of history
>
> But nevertheless
> despite the high priests of our shame
> we dwell on dying
> martyrs
> of our dreams
> > ("Screaming Against Tomorrow's Silence," p. 105)

Léonard Forest published two volumes during the 1970's: *Saisons antérieures* in 1973 and *Comme en Florence* in 1979. In his first collection, especially, the reality of Acadie is no less present than in the work of Forest's contemporaries, but it is more discreet and blurred by a rich screen of symbols, illustrating a poetic culture more firmly rooted in tradition. The mystery of his poetry, however, gives back in deferred strength what is lost in immediate clarity. Like Ronald Després, Léonard Forest was clearly influenced by poets of France, as he shows in this wink to Ronsard:

> parmi la semaine morose
> que nulle espérance n'arrose
> nos désirs privés de soleil
> n'attendent que l'heure sacrée

où l'émoi d'une joie pourprée
flambera, au matin pareil.

(amid a week, a dour cast
when nothing waters hope, at last
our wants, our sunlight all forlorn
wait only for that holy hour
when the joy, a scarlet flower
will flaming glow in the same morn.)
(from *Saisons antérieures*)

or in the rhyming verses of "Itineraries":

you imagine me aspiring to rhyme,
already drunk with shocking words that ring
at the end of lines whose loud thunders bring
both the proof and the brilliance of the crime.
("Itineraries," p. 98)

Gérald Leblanc is, without a doubt, the poet who unites the poets of the 1970's with those of the 80's. A writer whose work appeared in the pages of the periodical *L'Acayen* at the most militant moment of Acadian nationalism, he is, today, both the driving force behind the poetic activity in Moncton and the most prolific of Acadian poets, with three volumes of poems appearing between 1984 and 1988. Incarnating the figure of the poet with a cause, Gérald Leblanc carries to its paroxysm a cry of revolt against all the oppressors, whether they be American imperialists, anglosaxon bosses or the Acadian establishment. But Gérald Leblanc also leads the way to post-modernism and the explosion of all the rules:

your words return in the stillness: "We shall see
each other, we shall dream each other." i dream in
your mouth, i dream in your body. because love
looks like you. because *can, talmak, ulak*. because a
current is passing. because the season goes forward.
because the earth turns. because we are turning with
it.
("January Stillness," p. 114)

In the 1970's, the absence of a literary tradition allowed Acadian poets to write with great freedom. As Alain Masson notes:

> There is no such thing as a literary heritage in Acadie; literature is a project, a plan. Paradoxically, the Acadian writer thus finds himself right in the middle of universality . . .
> The values of a work cannot be confronted with models here, but must be deduced from their individuality itself.[2]

Ignoring the metre of French verse, with which they hardly concerned themselves, Acadian poets bypassed and even overturned the rules of their art, giving themselves the freedom to write, at various times, in good French, in poor French, in "chiac" or even in English, variations that, unfortunately, run the risk of being lost in translation. Coming to literature late and empty-handed has its advantages. Being open to outside influence and keeping a distance from literary canons allowed Acadian poets to enter into post-modernism as if they invented it.

At the beginning of the 1980's, Acadian poetry made a decisive turn away from nationalist themes and today the poetry of Acadie is crossed by the major currents of world literature: feminist writing, the rejection of rational and aesthetic restrictions, minimalist prose, fantasy and dream. If Acadian literature is still a regional literature — and today there is nothing pejorative in this description — it is no longer regionalist. Moreover, the "Acadian" label is no longer given simply to work of a more or less folkloric variety; rather Acadian poetry is most discernable in the particular manner by which it transforms writing practices. But this transition from a nationalist literature to one with universal preoccupations has not always been easy: for certain writers, such as Herménégilde Chiasson, the state induced by the consciousness-raising of the 1970's is a lost paradise; for readers inside and outside the community, the image of the whining Acadian is reassuring and, for critics, exoticism is so often attractive.

But the new Acadian poets have made their choice and they are not looking back. Gathering around the omnipresent Gérald Leblanc, sup-

---

2   Alain Masson, "Étranglement Étalement," in *Si Que I, Revue de l'Université de Moncton*, Vol. 7, no. 2, May 1974, p. 167.

ported by the remarkable returns of Guy Arsenault, Raymond LeBlanc and Herménégilde Chiasson, they seem determined to make better and better use of their particular freedom. Their poetry, like much of contemporary poetry, moves in the infra-reality of a deliberately banal everyday existence, attempting to reconstruct its infinitesimal movements — the outlines of a gesture or the flicker of a sensation, as, for example, in the poems of Roméo Savoie:

> you take my arm in your two hands
> you squeeze yourself very hard so you won't be afraid
> as for me, I pretend
>
> ("The Crowd," p. 168)

At the other extreme, there is an interest in fantasy and dream, particularly pronounced in the work of Dyane Léger where the everyday world can lurch into one which is outrageously imaginary, where cars and goldfish, St. Paul de Kent and Mexico, the Infant Jesus and French fries slide together. This poetry makes language explode into fireworks, dispersing its effects as far as possible. The shock induced by the work of Rose Després comes out of the constant play of continuity and discontinuity:

> Geographical recollections, the regions of my heart
> reach as far as the excited passageways...
> Children...Lingalan chatter...waves in the first
> person plural, my sense in prison
> and our radioactive exchanges swell up between us
> in illicit reflections.
>
> ("At the Star-port," p. 73)

In Louis Comeau's writing, emotion is evoked in spite of a language on the verge of rupture:

> Teaching me the one truly necessary thing, SUFFER-
> ING, without brilliance, a burn, a cut, a break, a bill
> of sale, drink, fish, passion, prison.
>
> ("To My Father," p. 59)

The provocative refusal to submit to the conventions of traditional poetry is combined, in these poems, with a rejection of politeness and euphemism in erotic discourse, often leading to the scatalogical, where both literal and literary expression flourishes.

Acadie also witnessed, during the 1980's, the rise of many women writers who ensured over half of its poetic production and who largely shaped its poetry throughout the decade. Dyane Léger, Huguette Légaré, Rose Després, France Daigle, Anne Cloutier and Huguette Bourgeois, without relying on feminist militancy, give Acadian writing a particular mark, quite different from the canonical models for literature toward which they have always been told they could never aspire.

In the 1980's, America occupied a privileged position for the contemporary poetry of Acadie, giving rise to cultural references and inspiring rhythms, syntactical divisions, syncopated sequences that form an original hybrid of the American "beat" translated into French words. Gérald Leblanc, in *Geographie de la nuit rouge*, offers a number of examples of this Acadian-American fusion.

Yet Acadians also occupy a special position with relation to the overwhelming presence of the Americans. Unlike English Canadians, Acadians are not afraid of losing their identity to America: in fact, they represent a breach in American uniformity. Unlike the Québécois, America does not pose problems of communication for the bilingual Acadian, and like their French-speaking neighbors in Québec, Acadians welcome their privileged position in North America as a way of distinguishing themselves from European "Frenchness." Acadians thus use their "Frenchness" to resist America and use their "Americanness" to resist the hegemony of French culture. Certainly, this is a risky game and only time will tell the results.

Having left behind its regionalism, Acadian poetry became more diversified in the 1980's, making room for works which are original and sometimes atypical, from the old-fashioned charm of Robert Pichette's poems and the undefinable writing of France Daigle, neither prose nor poetry, yet resolutely narrative and poetic, to the experience of Roméo Savoie whose writing is inspired by his own paintings. Nor is Acadie as monolithic as one might think. It has opened its doors to non-Acadians such as Huguette Légaré, Gérard Étienne, Henri-Dominique Paratte and Roseann Runte, who have shared with Acadian poets their perspective on the world and their literary work. Acadian poets also count among their ranks Maurice Raymond, a master of the French language who can carve out new images over twenty or thirty verses as smoothly as a tightrope walker. If in the midst of post-modernism, Acadian poetry can offer poetry written in a classic style, with a trace of Mallarmé in its quest for poetic absolutes, what other surprises has it reserved for the future?

After twenty years of existence, it is, of course, too early to take inventory of Acadian poetry, to make final judgments. This is all the more true because Acadian literature is fundamentally a literature that is anti-literary and anti-formalist, in the process of inventing a new code. It would be futile to apply old criteria. Yet, it is not because of its individual authors but because of its very existence that Acadian poetry is important today. It is unique in the sense that no other literature has had such an impact on the collective consciousness of a people; no other one has been given such a responsibility; no other literature has benefitted from such freedom or participated so intrinsically in the rebirth of a nation.

For the moment, Acadian poetry seems to be enjoying good health. The literary institution has been strengthened by the creation of two or three publishing houses. Acadian literature is taught as a legitimate subject in universities both in Acadie and elsewhere. The Association des écrivains acadiens has published the 15th issue of *Éloizes*, a journal of Acadian writing, and participated in a number of exchanges with the Union nationale des écrivains québécois. Work by Acadian poets now appears in such Québec journals as *La Nouvelle Barre du Jour, Lèvres urbaines* and *Estuaire* — and this is only the visible proof of contacts between Acadian poets and those of the Québec avant-garde grouped around Yolande Villemaire and Claude Beausoleil. Most importantly, the number of publications has steadily increased: between 1980 and 1990, more than thirty volumes of Acadian poetry were published. Although this figure may seem small to a larger community, it is substantial when one realizes that the only francophone daily newspaper in the Maritimes has never sold more than 15,000 copies.

At the same time, the society from which this poetry emerges has become increasingly complex and multivocal. And the future, if not threatened, is unpredictable. What is certain is that the voice that was heard at the beginning of the 1970's has never stopped speaking. With this anthology, Acadian poetry establishes special links which join Acadians to their anglophone neighbours. Thanks to the publishers and editors of this volume, the barrier has finally been crossed.

RAOUL BOUDREAU

GUY ARSENAULT

Born in Moncton in 1954, Guy Arsenault wrote the poems in his first published collection between the ages of 14 and 18. He now works full-time on his poetry and painting.

Publications: *Acadie Rock* (Éditions d'Acadie, 1973), *Poèmes et Dessins* (6 chapbooks published by the Author, 1979-1981), *Y'a toutes sortes de personnes* (Michel Henry Éditeur, 1989).

To Celebrate September

A garden ripened
from a summer without spring
and without autumn

I see again and again
the fishermen return from the sea
I drink again and again
of earth's solitude
from their work-worn hands
I drink again and again
out of their faint
and faded eyes
of peace reflected from the sea
I drink again and again their poetry

A summer ripened
from a garden without flowers
a summer ripened
from a garden without fruit

I am eager
I display
my changes of colour
I gather in my fruit
from my summer garden
I cool down
I shorten my days
I am eager

And the colour
and the freshness
and the chill
of September
give us a warning:
it's there in the air
it's there in the weather
it's there in the earth
it's there in the sea
Red!!
    . . . the wild Summer
of an October uprising!

Backyard Tableau

mosquito bites
banana peel
bottle cap
pod borer
popsicle stick
potato bug
. . . as if everybody knew everybody else

peppermint garden
fence
apple core
bottle with a hole in the cover for trapping *japs*
broken *clothespins*
marbles
dirt road
stolen rhubarb tastes better than rhubarb not stolen
pot for *marbles*
tag you're it
. . . as if everybody didn't know everybody else

dandelions
to make necklaces and bracelets and to find out
   whether or not we like butter
nun's buns
Leblanc's old shed

tar paper
nobody's big rats
tar paper
sticking out from under Leblanc's old shed
my Aunt Rosella's *cookies*
Pépère has gone on a drunk again
the cat has eaten my collection of dead flies
black *candy*
... as if everybody knew everybody else

church bells
first communion
holding hands
... Denise ...
... Anne-Marie ...
hide and seek
sneakers
church bells
"It's six o'clock. We have to go in and say the
    rosary."
nun's convent
holy pictures
smell of a nuns' convent
Sunday clothes
... as if everybody didn't know everybody else

Sunday afternoon picnics
after vespers
by the first stream
along the telephone poles
and taking the narrow path
going by the new houses
going by Jimmy Budd's
or taking the road from the *pit* or by the *piggery*
Sunday afternoon picnics
after vespers
by the first stream

relatives from the States
with uncle Archie and his whisky
and his American beer

Budweiser
relatives from Québec
with uncle Franco
and his spaghetti dishes
and his kids sticky with *popsicles*
. . . as if everybody didn't know everybody else

first class altar boy
big paten-man
a true acolyte
30 cents a week
It's my turn to serve the 8 o'clock mass
with my cassock
and my surplice
I was comfortable
I could feel important as well
turning down the cloth on the communion rail
I could feel important
emptying a cruet full of wine into Father Pellerin's
    chalice
. . . three drops of water and a lot of wine
I could feel important
when I had to serve all by myself
or when I was in church
and someone else was serving all by himself
and the priest beckoned us from the sanctuary
just before mass
with just time enough to pull on any old cassock or
    surplice
and to catch up with them at the Kyrie
or at the epistle if it was Father Pellerin
that guy only took twenty minutes to say a mass
and then there were the funerals
with tall candles
and Sunday afternoon vespers
with monstrance and censer

midnight mass
a little
wispy
snow

falling softly
right
before the church door as far as our house
and the meat pies
and Christmas presents
and the hockey scores
Christmas stockings stuffed with Christmas *candies*
and Christmas cooking
and making the rounds at Christmas
and the smell of Christmas
and Christmas morning
calm
clear
true
serene
and Christmas afternoon
with relatives from Scoudouc
Alyre and Stella and their family
with relatives from Shédiac
godfather and godmother
with relatives from Parkside
Alphée and Lina and their family
Merry Christmas
Christmas with the family
Christmas with no family
Merry Christmas and a Happy New Year
a funny year
marked by celebrations, vacations, and religious
    obligations
so that no one gets bored
and then there's Lent
a long Lent without *candy*
with mass every day
and the stations of the cross on Saturdays
wearing our Winter boots until Resurrection Day
and Spring . . .
Holy Week
Easter duties
Pentecost
Palm Sunday
no time to be bored when you're an altar boy

and then there's the Corpus Christi procession
on *Mountain Road*
beginning at the Church
passing in front of the *Post Office*
as far as *Al's Variety*
going down Lefurgey
crossing the traffic on Connaught
passing in front of Cooper's house
in front of Thériault's house
passing in front of the field where we played
    baseball with a sponge ball and a good board
    without splinters
on Summer evenings
Spring evenings
and Fall evenings
arriving at last at Verdun school
where we knelt down on the hard gravel
to put up with the litanies of the Blessed Virgin
and the litanies of St. Anne
and the litanies of all the saints
and be submitted to the exposition of the Blessed
    Sacrament
for about ten minutes
long enough to redden our knees
and we went back to the church
down Chester
passing in front of our own house
and in front of Catherine's store
and in front of Leblanc's, Haché's, Lirette's and
    Léger's
in order to get back to the street corner
where we went up Churchill
as far as the church
At the head the monstrance and the Host
(out on display since Easter)
followed by the parish priests
followed by the assistant priests
followed by all the altar boys
followed by all the members of Lacordaire
followed by all the ladies of St. Anne

followed by all the members of the St. Vincent de
    Paul Society
followed by all the Boy Scouts
followed by all the Cubs
followed by all the Girl Guides
followed by all the Crusaders
followed by all the junior Crusaders
followed by all the executive of the Recreation club
followed by all the members of the Caisse populaire
followed by all the parishioners . . .
. . . as if every one knew every one else

model student
first prize for the highest average twice
second prize for the second highest average twice
prize for greatest progress during an academic year
at the presentation of prizes at the Verdun school
end of June 1961, '62, '63, '64.

row by row
in a straight line
on time (for what?)
row by row
Three cheers for recess
Three cheers for free time
Three cheers for vacations

dandelion fields
barbecues
a sea of salt water, sand, shells, *jelly fish* and the
    sunburns
of pretty girls, with bare legs, bums, and bodies
    stretched out on the sand
thunder rolls
and the weather turns gloomy
backyard
the smell of home
kitchen table
nun's buns
beef stew

the smell of home
my father's smell
my mother's smell
my sisters' smell and my brother's
my grandfather's smell
my own smell
the smell of home
as if everybody knew everybody else
backyard

The Wharf

wooden planks nailed
tarred
salted
worn with age by the sea

sun
twinkling streams
shifting
wrinkling
of calm waters in Bouctouche Bay

and the cold sea wind
got to him
and made him
feel
deeply

shadow on the ground
of a seagull sun
cry of a poet sitting
on the planks of the wharf
at Bouctouche Bay

earth-salt
sea-wind
seagull-sunlight
my arms enfold you

and the blades of grass
pushing out of the tarred
planks of the wharf
receive the caresses
of the sea breeze

and the blue sky shows only
a few traces of clouds on the horizon

the sea is pleased with it
and makes it known
and the poet
sitting on the tarred
planks of the wharf
embraces all

Writer's Block

Sometimes
intending to write
a poem
I repeat one phrase:
"Nothing written"
every thirty seconds.
Sometimes
I repeat it
like that
for days.
"Nothing written"
for days.

Women

women
fallen leaves
rain outdoors
your belly

I crawl in order to learn
in order to know you
I meet you
the day goes on
for both of us
everything is splendid
under this skin-cover

We Can't

We can't
forever live
in *I should have*
or in
if only things had happened that way
as if about to lose the advantages
of our former life
We can't
always
loaf around in the past
and pine in futility
to have it changed

GEORGES BOURGEOIS

A fisherman by trade, Georges Bourgeois is a native of Grande-Digue, New Brunswick. His poetry has been published in *Éloizes* and one of his short stories has appeared in *Concerto pour huit voix*, a collection published by Les Éditions d'Acadie in 1989.

Publications: *Les Îles Fidgi dans la baie de Cocagne* (Éditions Perce-Neige, 1986).

Myself With A Sharp Knife

Myself with a sharp knife
I made a huge gash in the belly of Summer,
plunged my hands into it to pull out its boiling heart

and getting up again all smeared with its blood,
imbued with its living and regenerating powers,
I felt beating inside me the secret pride
of a poacher.

Poem In Monochrome
To Denise, my sister

The dreary weather paints grey
the faces and fields of snow-covered villages
where only the echoes of a barking dog
(at Winter's door)
seem to break up the sad stillness
of these houses closed
on dwellers at the edge of the sea.

Little grey birds are clinging
to the dry branches of a dead apple tree
in a schoolyard accommodating
dreamy-eyed little pupils at their desks
half-asleep in front of tall window frames
and beautiful landscapes of frost.

The sky darkens a little and it's going to snow;
laboriously the big black overcoat of a widow
carrying her armload of wood crosses
the yard in front of the sagging and untidy shed
adjacent to
a copse of fir and dark green spruce.

Below, on the ice along the seashore
some tar-paper shacks with blue-smoke stove-pipes
hiding human beings
with faded woollen mittens
rounded on bottles of golden whiskey.

On the horizon-line
a tiny point approaches in the whitish bay:
it is a solitary fisherman moving away from
the stakes of his trap

> walking back, taking it easy
> followed by his faithful sledge
> and the dark.

Ode To The Mackerel Fishers

We are nomads,
    sea gypsies.
We come from St. Something, a tiny coastal village
completely ravished by a tidal wave:
we are villagers adrift,
our blue-violet mussel shells
make up this flotilla of toys
all rigged out in masts and sails
that splash about in a green field of waves.

Our days are fat and lazy;
on the morning breeze a floats soporific spirit
that aquatic plants exhale generously;
midday and we become sea wolves yawning in the
   dry land's sun
and in the evening, a pack that brightens up with
   fire-water.

Then from midnight to dawn,
that is when we become a race of guillemots
always on the lookout over our ice fields;
fishing is our salvation.

Though they call us a tribe of Canadians,
         of Norwegians,
         or Icelanders,
we are in a way
primitives out of *The National Geographic*.
Satisfied, proud, and elusive,
our world remains unruffled
in front of the Queen Elizabeth all lit up
that sails by on the horizon.

We are the heroes
of an obscure and ordinary poet;
on a stormy night
we are no more than a spray of wood chips
tossed on the sea of your island.

HUGUETTE BOURGEOIS

Huguette Bourgeois, born in Rogersville, New Brunswick in 1949, won the Prix France-Acadie in 1988 for *L'Enfant-fleur*; a new collection of her poetry, *Espaces libres*, is forthcoming from Les Éditions d'Acadie.

Publications: *Les Rumeurs de l'amour* (Éditions Perce-Neige, 1984), *L'Enfant-fleur* (Éditions d'Acadie, 1988), *Espaces libres* (Éditions d'Acadie, forthcoming).

Mutilations

The blackbirds chastise their dreams
At nightfall
Under the cramped forests of their lives
While hope and its funeral train
        lie assassinated

Dogs, Men And Women

Dogs go astray in the dark
Men also —
Sometimes women . . .

Landscape

just your hand
and the dazzling sweep of your glance
that is enough for illumination
that is illumination

If

the fracturable surface of your eyes
suddenly broken
could let one see
    the sea . . .

Here In This Room

here in this room
the shadow passes
the door opens in the dark
and a lamp keeps watch
your face has become dim
between us two
air
a faded memory
and hands search

in the void
for desires
that do not exist

Adieu

Later in the woods
    mingled voices
a few words
on the wind
that descends in the night
the rest follows . . .
    a prayer
one last leap of the heart
one bright
light . . .
but behind
pale forms complain
words
that I will not have said

Rain-Refrain

lovers of the air ruined
by all things that hang heavy
and drag on in the night
that howls and settles in

little lovers of the night
of nothing and of fortuitous
space

little lovers for a laugh
in the haziness
of silence

HERMÉNÉGILDE CHIASSON

Born in 1946 in St-Simon, New Brunswick, Chiasson is well known in Acadie as a filmmaker, playwright, visual artist and poet. He received a Master of Fine Arts from S.U.N.Y. and a doctorate from the Sorbonne where he completed a thesis on contemporary American photography.

Publications: *Mourir à Scoudouc* (Éditions d'Acadie, 1974), *Rapport sur l'état de mes illusions* (Éditions d'Acadie, 1976), *Précis d'intensité* (with Gérald Leblanc, *Lèvres urbaines* #12, 1985), *Prophéties* (Michel Henry Éditeur, 1986).

Between The Season Of Extravagant Love And The Season Of Raspberries

You went away opening cracks in the April ice that melted so fast, without noticing the spring as it hastened to come that year with a moist March wind sticking the leaves to their trees.

And you went away so fast that a part of me was exiled within you; you went away by roads among water puddles, mudholes, gaping wounds in the asphalt bleeding dirty water over our white clothes.

And I asked myself whether I would end up crossing the pale grass of burnt-over clearings and the fresh water of thaws in the voyage I took without a return ticket to see a garden of untroubled flowers.

There were cabbages growing nearby, and they gave me a bouquet of salad. Dusk fell and cars plunged into the darkness with all the racket of refugees reaching the border.

I closed the garden door again. A bouquet of Everlastings had been put on the table. I opened the door of the house once again and outside the raspberries had begun to ripen.

So That You Can't Fly Away

You have eyes like birds that are going to fly away. I would like to write you with new words to hear myself say in a new tongue that I want to learn to speak once again the language of green-feathered birds, to tell you to spread out paradise, to push with both hands against the clouds that shrink the sky, to cut out a sun for every day; to speak to you as if you were the last word I had left to say; to take your heart in both of my hands to keep it in your body, to keep it from getting cold so that you won't fly away; to tell you with words as warm as your body what we will call each other when there are no more words between us and you are my most beautiful bird wheeling around a white sun over a white stream; to create a spring for you like a great field of just-ripe strawberries, so that you can settle down and make your nest under the birches. And the clouds working loose from the sky will make the rain in my eyes, because you have eyes like birds that are going to fly away.

All The King's Horses

All the king's horses have died together, my love.
All the king's horses have died in the blue stream.
But from the bottom of my stream, crushed beneath
the horses' bodies, I got up and marched, carrying the
harness of my dead horse.

All the king's horses have died together, my love, in
the big blue stream. But there was no longer a king to
own the streams. Kings had forgotten that they were
kings, they had forgotten that they were alone, and
that without love they were going to die with their
horses that had fallen asleep, never to waken again.
That, I believe, was yesterday.

All the king's horses have died and we are dead too.
We have slipped in the water on the cold soft hair of
stretched and gutted black horses bleeding red in the
blue of the stream.

Eugénie Melanson

Neither necklaces of fresh water
Nor flaming censers that priests hold aloft during
Corpus Christi
Nor Good Friday banners
Nor tricolour flags
Nor lost loves
Nor loves permissible, still
Will have made your beauty fade, Eugénie Melanson
You whose photo came down through the years
To signal me
One June afternoon when the sky was too blue and as
the sun was setting too low in a country that could no
longer be mine.
You were the loveliest, all the same.
Others will have told you that, I know, but I imagine
your dark wide-open eyes that looked inside your

body so as to no longer see the years pass over your forgotten beauty.

You were the loveliest, all the same

When you disguised yourself as Évangéline in order to recreate with Gabriels on parade the memorable dates of an inglorious past, swallowed up in the dreams and poems of yesteryear that you had never read.

You were the loveliest, all the same

When one Sunday afternoon a wandering photographer caught the freshness of your eighteen years and fixed, by a slow painful process, the faulty remains of an incredible candour, the slow and almost dark dream of a desire to stay now and forever watching the sun dimming itself in the sky for one last time, yes, for just one last time.

You were the loveliest, all the same

Because one Sunday afternoon that photo came into existence and one afternoon in June, your presence looked at me and made me pause.

You were looking out from behind your picture frame, from above your black dress, your face against the glass

You were watching, although deep within your body, your eyes no longer looked.

You were watching, Eugénie Melanson, I know, you were watching

Blue showcases, pious objects, lace-edged cradles, axes fastened into the workbench, ploughs that no longer turn the sod, the Victorian furniture of folk who were richer than you were, do you remember, the gas lanterns that blinked near the door when, on windswept autumn evenings, your young men had just brought you home, leading you as far as the steps, you saw fireplaces with real birch fire-logs, you who had always dreamed of it, do you remember, you looked at sleighs bounding on the snow on Sunday afternoons when there were vespers at church and when, muffled up in furs, you thought you were going to midnight mass in broad daylight . . .

You saw all that, Eugénie Melanson, but all the same . . .

All the same, you were lovelier than all the dreams that were flattened against the glass by a June day when, here, as on all other June days, nothing happened.

You were lovelier than the Vatican medals that went to the dignitaries whose names your husband sometimes mentioned and whose pictures you sometimes saw in the papers.

And today . . .

Today all of you are here

You are imprisoned, yourself, the Vatican medals, the picture of the Expulsion, Monsignor Richard's linen flag, and all the dreams that live behind the glass of this great cage for nostalgia.

You are at the end of a corridor and you watch the children coming to look at the blue showcases who do not notice your small photo lost in its black and white.

But you are the loveliest, Eugénie Melanson, lovelier than Philomène LeBlanc, lovelier than Valentine Gallant, lovelier than Euphrémie Blanchard smiling on the arm of Evariste Babineau, lovelier than the Vatican medals, Champlain's signature, and the wax seals of the kings of England, France, and Spain.

You are the loveliest because I love you

Because you did not know the Gibson girls, nor the suffragettes, Barnum's Circus, the Beverley Follies, the Wright brothers, nor Thomas Edison and because you fell asleep near lace-edged cradles.

You should have awakened.

You should have awakened since that was when the desire to die clutched your body.

You should have awakened, Eugénie Melanson

But you fell asleep in your body

While thinking of blue showcases, Champlain's signature, the Fort at Beaubassin, the cannons of the French ships opening fire as they came into port at Île Saint-Jean . . .

You fell asleep

You fell asleep while dreaming

You fell asleep while dreaming of new expulsions.

Blue

Acadie is no more. There's no longer a black boat in the sea with white sails gliding on the water, our sea, our Atlantic, our desire to glide to the world's end, but we are at the world's end. There's no longer a blue sailboat like the one in which my father spent half of his life between the blue of the sky and the blue of the sea. And I would stop writing if I didn't know that the one hope of seeing a new crew is the one already taking form in the eyes of my father who is setting sail in his own Acadie that is farther away than mine, an Acadie that's no longer a hell but a desire to take down the axes from the barn walls and to say that's enough, we have reached the end of the world, we have to bury it or be buried ourselves. And I have begun to wonder if one day this crew will take to the sea with the sun inside it, if one day this crew will take to the sea before my mother who prays to blue madonnas for my white sins and does not want to see red blood on white snow nor a black flag in the blue sky, my mother with her fingernails broken from too much digging in the earth and who may have already learned to say *PLEASE*.

Red

Acadie, my too beautiful desecrated love, you whom I will never take into white sheets, the sheets that you have torn to make white flags like the fields of snow that you have sold like your old fence posts, your old barns, your old legends, your old dreams, white as an old wedding dress in an old cedar chest. Acadie, my too beautiful desecrated love, who speaks on credit to say things that one must pay in cash, who borrows privileges while believing she is gaining rights. Acadie, my too beautiful desecrated love, on *stand-by* on every continent, on *stand-by* in every galaxy, divided by church steeples that are stretched too thin, filled with saints up to a heaven that is too far away. Rip off your blue dress, put red stars on your breasts, sink yourself

into the sea, the red sea that is going to open as it did
for the flight from Egypt, the sea belongs to us, it is
true, the whole sea belongs to us because we cannot
sell it, because there is no one who could buy it.

Plain

I saw the non-existence and at the same time the
delirious sense of your marvelous presence
in a public place impregnated with light.
They say it is the size, the surface
that ends up modifying the idea of heat,
of sunlight, if you prefer.
Something vast and fuzzy
like the unusual presence of the sea
in the recesses of the earth.

I would have liked to have known you in a foreign
land where men dance together
to the worldly beat of destitution
to the music of revolt and unheard-of contingencies.

On the sand, soldered together in the opaque mass of
darkness, abandoned to these foreign lands,
there would be no more fields, no more borders,
only a scent.
A vague scent in the wind of an eternal Winter.
The plain belongs to a dry and careless world
where the shore recaptures its magical splendour
as it enjoys squandering all our perspectives.

(sic)

You spoke of oppression and I took notes.
One never knows.
I wrote down your dreams like a stratagem,
an intricate web defying provisional freedom
and good fortunes in respite.
I was afraid of forgetting the deep-seated reasons

that had made of your bad luck an inconsistent
parameter for measuring the ocean of misunder-
standings that unfurled between us.

And your heart started to beat again at the centre of
suspicion, a submarine conflagration, an ecosystem
that upset all the radars.

That day we bought new clothes
and we were eager to get our visas,
barometers of a certain amount of banality.
The border was close at hand.
You didn't even dare to mention it.
You were content to sign
while throwing in a few old curses
which did not even make an impression.
People who knew of your bad temper
even surprised themselves by telling you how
desirable and blameless you were from then on.
You have done nothing to prove them wrong.
I shall always resent you for that.
I shall always resent you, believe me.

Constellation

Stars of gold . . .
Ah the beautiful stars like luminous points
for nailing the sky onto the pillars of the night . . .
Stars of gold . . .
Ah the beautiful stars that turn their sinister
tips, enchantment or dust sail
on the magic carpet of the night . . .
Stars of gold . . .
Ah the beautiful stars, you who become pale
like so many geneses, undreamt-of
in the futile need to be unique, narrow stairway
to climb in the dizzying shadows
right up to the arches of the night . . .

Stars of gold, and I, I sleep
in the silence of their gigantic voyage,
inventing depths for myself
where time no longer has a price and boredom no
    more power.

ANNE CLOUTIER

Anne Cloutier was born in Edmundston on September 27, 1963. Her poetry has been published in *Éloizes, Lèvres urbaines* and other magazines. She has studied Comparative Literature and now lives in Montréal where she works as a free-lance writer and critic.

Publication: *Popor Manne* (published by the Author, 1983).

Detour   Return
And   IN THE TROPICS

springing from nocturnal vapours   the velvet
moist glidings   of heels on the sidewalk   bursting
the post-partum blues   like a St. Catherine Street
without passers-by   at six o'clock in the morning   a
double white line waiting glowing as far as infinity   a
dragonfly splitting the light's milky orb   a fly on the
bars of an electric veil   resisting numbness   trying
a first...second...eleventh step step step step
sixteenth floor hoarse gasps   we open with difficulty
this window and the weight of the effort at the end
of drowsy arms   opened with difficulty this
window   reflecting an orange blade furrowing the
sky   it yawns   in the rise of daylight   how can
one tell what is promised   that probably would
most likely have been   like a jagged tear-line in
curtain lace   beaten by a squall subjected to bad
weather   timeless   bad times   I have spent the
night lying under your tongue   and however that
was   wasn't it   you   not   me   who would have
had the desire to   devour and be devoured and finally
she be devoured   another passer-by   passes (and)

Picture Us There

the intensity of a doubt   one alone   breaks up the
layers of dark   and stillness   an unexpected visi-
tor   throws at our feet its black cape   heavy   so
heavy   and who knows whether we will not
leave tomorrow in another bus with punctured
tires   searching if in the margins of our memories
we might have glued a polaroid of both of us soldered
together at the chest   making bruises on our neck
one last time   fingers twisted   in the keenness
conscious   of desire

> IN A CERTAIN FRAME OF MIND
> imagining still
> in the pallor of my flesh
> the lens of your gaze
> burning

In A Room . . .

In a hotel room. On a bed, she, stretched out. A chair
from which the other listens. End of the afternoon.
April. She speaks. She speaks words that fall like
broken glass. Gestures, colours reconstituted from a
long passage through voices. Penetration of words.
Speech taken up and then left. Dying, there. The
window takes back the reach of arm wandering toward
table. Here, cigarettes, enclosed in dark rectangle,
matchbox square. Light. Deep inspiration. Moist
exhalation. Diffusion of brownish particles in the
saturated air. Flexing of the wrist. Return of the
cigarette. Painful flexing. Pain like a habit. With each
movement. Whether from there or elsewhere. A June
morning. The sky heavy with its blueness, with its
contained heat. In the apple tree, its branches dusty.
Tumult of flowers and birds. On a branch, she, seated.
Watching the sun melt, stretch out, and leak drop by
drop into her eyes, until there is only a silvery infinity.
Fallen again from her eyelids, veiling with red the

underlying burn. Passage to darkness. Blinking of
eyelashes. Rotation of the iris, eye staring downwards.
At the foot of a tree, the child plays at watching the
grass grow. The sky's turbulence. Dizziness. Beginning
of the fall. Sucked in by the whirlwind, suddenly. Fall
begun. Nausea rising again in the throat. Fall. The
child was watching the grass grow. Incessantly, she, her
steps around the bed. Smoke sways in the over-heated
air. Bitter peace. Recalling the scorched-mitten smell of
heater. Out-of-date fires. But — another hotel. A few
times, footsteps in the corridor, too. Unknown faces
on the other side of the wall. Pause. She goes to the
window. Presses her forehead against it. On the outer
surface of the glass, ridges of water and soot.
Interfering with perception. A drop to the second floor
of the town. A sphere defined by its carbonized dome.
Hazy clouds. Multiple, multiplied, sky-lines smutty
with house tops. Billboards whose language overhangs
the signs of daily life. Against the window spatters of
reality. And what if from all that vision was twisted.
From that which, through fragments, should expose a
story. Precisely. It was the child. *"Fant"* for *"feu."*
Yellow gleam of his ball bouncing on the pavement.
Still, dead birds lay scattered about the cement. In the
morning. Wings caked to their bodies. The shapes of
their flesh ordered by that of the hand holding them.
At the pressure of a finger, this hollowing of the
abdomen. He, watched with his absent-minded gaze,
an opening running toward the interior. A personal
film library. Watercolour images. Erased, a little. Like
the layout of the city perceived beyond this misted
window. Through rain, now. From the room, she
knows the smell of rain splashing on the sidewalk,
digging into ice. She talks about it, and her words fall
like shells that might have forgotten to burst. And
what if the story could be fused only through a
subversion of reality. A certain distribution of its
fragments. Pause. On the table, cigarettes. Light.
Inspiration. Exhalation. Flexing of the wrist. Return.
The child. It was *"Fant"* for *"feu."* One evening,
doesn't matter which. Alone, she listened. Cries

growing faint. Swelling in the heart of silence. Bewildered race to the appointed room. Escaping from the partly opened door the leprechaun flames. The child. Nested in a velvet hollow. A niche between two folds of the curtain, there. Its body so calm. Black hair flocked in his eyes. Green, moreover. Moreover, between the thumb and the index finger, screwed tight. A cigarette lighter of tarnished silver. Retrieved, afterward. Naptha juiced from the end of its tongue. Brandished like a sepulchral candelabra. From which sparks came. *"Fant"* for *"feu."* It was. Pressed to the window, she. Lets the words crumble; speech ripens to its slow death. From there, a single vision possible. A cloud where some thousands of yellow gleams burst. Burgeoning beneath the rain. This, only, remains. In the dark. Remains only the smoking smell of rain copulating with ice.

CLARENCE COMEAU

Clarence Comeau was born in Néguac and received his B.A. from the Université de Moncton in 1976. His first collection of poems, *Entre amours et silences*, received the Prix France-Acadie in 1981. His plays, *Première neige d'automne* and *Pour entendre rire les enfants*, have been broadcast on Radio-Canada. Clarence Comeau now resides in Montréal.

Publications: *Entre amours et silences* (Éditions d'Acadie, 1980), *Quelque part en nous ... Ton visage* (published by the Author, 1987), *Caresse obscure* (published by the Author, 1988).

Beside Your Lovely Fields ...

beside your lovely fields of clover
there was a child
with bare and muddy feet

beside your great fields of clover
a child who gazed at your beauty
and, filled with love, waited for the years

he used to watch you as he waited
to play in your great fields of clover

a child used to shiver as he imagined
hands on his beautiful young and soft
bottom . . . A belly that warmed up
his own beside your great fields of Summer

a child who waited to grow up
while laying out a landscape
a house
a tree
a fence
a river a bridge a sun
and a man who acted like a man

beside your great fields of clover
a child was guilty of loving you

he was wretched like children
like the man who acted like a man

beside your great fields of clover
my childhood trembled at the thought
of loving you when the swallows returned

Cries Of Love And Silence

1

No need for children

who speak the loneliness of shores
to the legendary foam

No need for children

who hide in dismal harbours
abandoned by their mothers

No need for children

when a bird is pulled and tugged
between four seasons and lifetimes
in the dreams of childhood

No need for children

in oceans lost and weeping
for freedom encaged

No need for children
in hearths that smoke-cure
tenderness

2

No need for laws

that tell stories calling youth to arms
in the hands of a corpse

No need for laws

that punish prisoners' pleasures
with insurgents' remorse

No need for laws

when the seed germinates thoughts
desires of the flesh haunted
by the noise of marching
in the night

No need for laws

that condemn life to the cemeteries
of ghostly seasons

No need for laws for the taboos
casting a spell over the future
of this country

3

No need for a country

that grows a child to be butchered
by the executioner's hands

No need for a country

that is built in the wound of a body
frightened by the sea

No need for a country

when childhood is flattened
between mornings and evenings of weather
in which warfare is the beloved
of their tides

No need for a country

that ages the dying foetus
in the ache of living

No need for a country for adults
who drain blood from
the heart's joy

4

No need for a tomorrow

that prolongs yesterday in the bullet-ridden
vacancies of Lent

No need for a tomorrow

which makes the animal savage in
the nocturnal arena of the sick

No need for a tomorrow

when lions are crowned
today incapable of
leaving the throne of
a carnival jungle

No need for a tomorrow

that restores to life youth
killed by its first amorous smile

No need for a tomorrow for loves
unsuited to believing
in Spring

LOUIS COMEAU

A poet, illustrator and filmmaker, Louis Comeau has published a number of texts in newspapers and literary journals including *Éloizes* and *Estuaire*. He was born in Free Grant, New Brunswick in 1955.
Publications: *Moosejaw* (Éditions Perce-Neige, 1981).

As If For Change...

Images no longer follow the rhythm of a rosary read
by an hysteric confined to the lavatories, with social
cramps, colic from the refusal to obey. And the long
reel suddenly takes form like a story repeated one
hundred times, each time more precisely, diminishing
to the point of renewal, the *jazz*, the *come*, the orgasm,
and its Christian feeling of impropriety which closes

the door on visceral sensations. I have seen impotence forming, changing, and I have been sick from wanting to challenge things. As if everything were happening elsewhere, as if the action had preceded us. I have been sick for challenge, as if for change.

Fear

The fear in my house.
Going out into long streets.
Wagging tongues.
Eyes on posts.
A streak of daylight over window casings
The evening above the aerials.
It is the fear of others that makes me afraid.

To My Father

Like an entrance in a gust of wind that smells of the winter cold and dirties the floor.
A fox *par excellence*, in the woods as in the town.
A war decoration (right in the parlour).
A story written between the lines of his discourse — our story — in the simple rhythm of his everyday movements. In every furrow of his old countenance, cut in the cold, sanded by the wind. A world in proportion to his axe, big as the sky, tiny as his teacup — chill and proper, unlucky, imbued with its smallness framed by blasphemies, pardonable blunders. Teaching me the one truly necessary thing, SUFFERING, without brilliance, a burn, a cut, a break, a bill of sale, drink, fish, passion, prison. A boat, a boot, the two holes, pissing upright, hands frozen in a world without mittens. As if BY CHANCE his wife, whose fingers know the exact road to move lovingly through his hair (a lesson in love) — An image which faded from our memories within two weeks — (are we no stronger than that?) — sometimes as painfully present as regret.

His regiment of nightmare wolfhounds is released from him to us. Not really humanitarian, more like duty. But what do I know about it.

It would be weariness,
the death of a tree,
a dried apple's wrinkles,
soured milk,
dread of being in a room by one's self,
fear of a shadow,
crying out loud, speaking very softly,
liking this, not liking that,
being a squabbler, not being one.

To my father, for his wisdom about the unchanging, about the useless, his awareness of having a tiny role to play — caretaker, forest ranger —

If I had all the dreams hidden behind his brow, all those ideas that come from his age (to be able to laugh at history), I would not feel like a coward for taking advantage of his death to obtain some fine turn of phrase, but I cannot meet death with him. If what did occur was a death, I myself saw it treated like a business by a malicious but respectable Christianity. I regret this ignorance. It was perhaps to get away from the mystery. But there is only mystery for those who close their eyes. For the rest of us, what remain are appreciation and its symbols.

FRANCE DAIGLE

France Daigle, born in Dieppe, New Brunswick in 1953, is an active member of the cultural community in Moncton. She works there as journalist and has published her work in a number of literary journals.

Publications: *Sans jamais parler du vent* (Éditions d'Acadie, 1983), *Film d'amour et de dépendance* (Éditions d'Acadie, 1984), *Histoire de la maison qui brûle* (Éditions d'Acadie, 1985), *Variations en B et K* (Éditions Nouvelle Barre du Jour, 1985), *L'été avant la mort* (with Hélène Harbec, Éditions Remue-ménage, 1986).

And It Went On

Then there was no more poetry, no more music,
    no more songs
There was only silence and the sound of motors.
There were no more raindrops trickling down
    the windows.
Then there were no more windows through which
    to see.
There were only a few scattered words that death
    had come to find
Then there was only the hand of these words, and
    then only the shadow of this hand
Then there was nothing left.
Nothing left to say, nothing left to do.
Pain had made itself at home between us and had
    taken up all the room.

It was as if in some shadowy past; something was
    dreary to display.
Maybe it was death, death of our dreams in the
    morning upon awakening.
Maybe it was life, life beyond dreams after
    death in the morning after awakening.
Maybe it was a little of all that but no one
    could say.
We did not know
It was mysterious and it did not go away

And then it went on and on.
As a story goes on, it went on a few years, a few
    centuries, a few hours.
It went on like a story told later on, much later on.
Like stories that are told late, very late in the night
    of our faded dreams.
It went on until the uncertain time of old age.
It went on.
There was nothing else to be done, and we did
    nothing more.
Death could come now to find us.

And it came.
Death came and got us.

Mediterranean Women

1

Hazy overhead, the afternoon
the other hand on a woman, plump and in black
her throat throbbing and desirous

low sky
classically still
waiting for it to pass

gloomy and smooth like what
always happens at the same time
the sea like the woman when she gets up
withdraws without warning
silent
lifeless
unfathomable
with the complexity of olives

2

what do I know about thinking of you
there where I loved you you did not know me
your wings (wide) above me
like restless shadows

rough drafts (rough ideas)
something inside
laughing or cooing
the too personal words of a letter
a flash
the clay echo of your footsteps
my inner workings when you pass

3

Each day each step towards you frightens and
    amazes me
laughing and progressive
(as if to carry it out one had to show confidence)
and too young for a heart so uprooted
(this city cannot be new even if it is rebuilt)
I move ahead, solemn and ridiculous
demanding that you have waited for me

4

on the roof of the shed
a robin is hunting for a place to fly
(maybe Greece)
the morning's cold light where already
Autumn is sounding the trees' retreat

on the other side of the street the forbidden chicken
    run
on the radio Nana Mouskouri sings of life
those who have ruled that hens should not live in
    town
those who have denied the hens access to the city

somewhere else children in nurseries
and, just as typical,
a rummage sale
(maybe Greece)

RONALD DESPRÉS

Ronald Després, born in Lewisville, New Brunswick in 1935, received second prize in the Concours littéraires de la province de Québec in 1959 and the Pascal Poirier Award in 1984. He now works as an interpreter in Ottawa.

Publications: Poetry: *Silences à nourrir de sang* (Éditions d'Orphée, 1958), *Les Cloisons en vertige* (Éditions Beauchemin, 1963), *Le Balcon des dieux inachevés* (Éditions Garneau, 1969), *Paysages en contre-bande . . . à la frontière du songe* (Éditions d'Acadie, 1974).

Fiction: *Le scalpel ininterrompu* (Éditions à la page, 1962).

Hymn To Spring

After deliberating in long whiteness
The fields decided not to wait for Easter
To have a resurrection.

A whip of fever lashes the forces of life
The thickets hurry to burst through their fallow
The little rivers to sacrifice their ice-sharks
On the greedy altars of the sun.

O kind filthiness of streets
You join in the same watercolour
The bourgeois paws of poodles
And the little faces of the slums!

Rooftops, gables, façades
Restore the alphabet of forbidden odours
The eaves have not finished
Letting the Arctic sift through
The song of gutters and thrushes drips
Into the ears of passers-by
Parted from their woollen layers.

The heart unmoved, at the crossing of seasons
The heart crushed beneath a false shell of joy
Tries again to find the miracle of petals
And the grace of the crocus that, already,
Is piercing the skin of the earth.

My Acadie
a poem in historical vignettes

My Acadie
a fragile vehicle for love
An Albatross of perfidious Sun-Kings
Belly stained by Abenakis
Brandy
Looking glasses for hides, feathers
And furs.

My Acadie
A mild messianic peasantry
Bras d'Or embracing
The Atlantis of our dreams
The rich silt of Minas Basin
At the porticos
Of the theatre of Neptune.

My Acadie
A shabby toy encased in seaweed
Gloomy majesty in deep mourning
North-South
Moving against the colonial dream
Between aimed guns in their emplacements.

My Acadie
Faithful tablecloth doubly secular
Scarcely cunning
Under the alien soup tureen
Nourished by repeated mirages
Of dense and credulous stillness
Like an age lulled to sleep.

My Acadie
Évangéline with velvet tread
With eyes repressing exile
Takes off her cowls of myth
And extends her arms to the newborn.

And cries out
— A strange likeness, lace torn —
Words tender
And awkward

AGAINST THE SALT TASTE OF BLOOD.

Poetry Night In Acadie

A borrowed land
Hung on memory's hanger
A fine showy cloak
Unravelled from the inside
By the ultimate betrayal
Of mute sleeves
And bowed shoulders.

A frozen land that fears the cold
Like a hotel bound by fog
That is loved and remembered
With gestures as sweeping as its shores
And with the names of heroes engulfed in it.

A land that is ours without being so
Made up of timid faces
Unacknowledged smiles
And impossible returnings.

A land like a parcelled-out mistress
Sharing even the beds of the mightiest
Even the repeated deceits
And the taste of hate upon awakening.

Then suddenly
A land consumed

By a long held-in fire
Of singing guitars
Heart-licking poems
And crowded elbows in the dream's
    half-light.

A land with warm curves
A land with its cloak of fog
Broken like bones
Beaten too long.

Suddenly
Naked without one shiver
A land of proud eyes
And clenched hands held out
Toward the light.

You are, my Acadie
— and this time without pain —
A land outward bound.

I Thought Of You All Day

I thought of you all day.

You were there, crouching behind every moment's
    dune
You were behind every door
And all doors stood wide open
To the theatre of the four winds.

I saw your brow, your lips, your hair,
Adorning the face of every passer-by
That I came across;
I saw your footsteps in every stride
Your hands in every prayer
And your voice in the stream of words.

I cried out for you to answer me, to smile at me
To tap me on the shoulder
But every time
You vanished from the reach of my voice
To be reborn elsewhere.

My day has taken root in you
Like a tree springing from nowhere
And see how its strange sap
Muddles the memory
That twilight brings to life in me.

I Loved You

I loved you
For the little cloud you nibbled unpretentiously
The sunlight that spilled into the nape of your neck
The sap that sprang either from you
Or from the flaming maples.

I loved you
For the mansion you bartered for my hut
Whose only furnishing was happiness
Decorating our bones and our bright walls.

I loved you
As a skeleton loves flesh
Or the sailor, salt water
And the vanished crews' sailboats
Silently soaking in the velvet of the waves.

I loved you
For your eyes
That echoed the horizon
For your teeth inviting ripe fruit
And your skin like a layer of sand
Over the shivers of your blood.

Suddenly, It Was Good To Be Alive

Suddenly, it was good to be alive
The sunlight's eyes punctured my blindness
Ushered in the bells and smells of a holiday
Filling the space of my refuge.

Suddenly, it was good to be alive
Clocks done away with
Winding-sheets transformed into festive tablecloths
Trees hastening to challenge Winter
To light up with flowers, fruits,
And birds on the point of nesting.

Suddenly
I had the sky in my attic
Reflecting the wonders of clear water
And every smile since the world began
Came to add lustre to your image.

Suddenly, it was good to be alive
For I had got you out of the picture frame
That binds you
Between the wall and my heart.

Hands

Those that open up like palm trees
Those that sneak deep into pockets
Those that show but one denouncing forefinger
Or knuckles clenched upon a cry.

Those that spread out like pools
To catch the sun-rays on their hair.

Those that plod on metallic fingers
From the casket's rust to the rusty tomb.

Those that erect monuments of solemn deeds
On pedestals larger than the world
And warmer than the heart.

Those that put in place of the horizon
Their own tormented contours
Whose bones make up the bars
Of their own prisons.

Those that speak farewells
Overwhelmed by ropes and dingy harbours
Those with small silken handkerchiefs
Embedded in the shifting sand of memory.

A workman's rugged hands
An old man's hands, hope-furrowed still
Those of a woman discovering her child's brows
To rest there lightly.

The dried-up hope in sidewalk beggars' hands
Hands that knead a hollow in a pillow
Roughing up and twisting and breaking to pieces
Abandoned faïence on the stall of happiness.

The bony hands of hunger
The earthy hands of war
The glittering hands of ballrooms
City hands that stick like glue.

And those of the poet,
Who, every evening, sets free new stars
And opens wide the shuttered panes of dream

In order that one day
All hands
Freed from the mirages of the flesh
Will take wing like birds
In a perfect blaze of palms joined together at last.

Your Footsteps

My overcoat, puffed out by wind,
Pitched its tent
Right in the circus of the streets.

And I, inside the tent,
I squeezed my grief with both hands
Like a panic-stricken dove.

Your steps withdrawing
Set drums beating
Broken gongs inside my temples.

I heard your steps, your steps, your steps
The steps of all the passers-by
Going, coming, moving away.

And my heart being crushed
Under each of them.

ROSE DESPRÉS

Rose Després is a writer, translator, teacher, actress and researcher. Born in Cocagne, New Brunswick in 1950, she has published her work in various journals and anthologies.

Publications: *Fièvre de nos mains* (Éditions Perce-Neige, 1982), *Requiem en saule pleureur* (Éditions d'Acadie, 1986).

Hymn To Light

A false sunshine has submerged my country in the holy wine where altar boys drown. Hosts are burning on the floor of the Father and of the Son, the realm of those who lower their heads at the sound of a sterile Monstrance, kissing the fear and the bishop's ring.

Pious stares like eagles pick at our brows, our guts and are blessed. Thanks to the intercession of a battered white bird, clumsily attached to the corner of a triangle where the celebrated all-powerful gaze is hidden, a path so narrow that even the blind hesitate to follow it while hurling insults to the stars, those hymns of molten lead that trickle down the dry vines of unsound contracts.

*

A sudden burst of silver thaw covers slumber, stifles the air with thick mist. Plants have not blossomed in their communion with time that sees the collapse of monotonous pendulums.

Universes of flame and silence are born in shadow-filled waters that jostle against inaccessible walls, knocking against the void, sweeping away the ashes of power and gathering the particles of unrest which surround it like moths under the spell of a lamp.

Tall windows open their magic eyes to the spectacle of a perpetual *mise-en-scène*; the roles encroach on a majestic decor, collections of made-up faces, blown-up on the winds of whirlpools.

And the children in the streets play at pricking balloons of illusions; they burst the shapes of many-coloured suns. On the cement carpet, the masks remain wizened and disappear with yesterday morning's fog.

*

Restrained, impatient, the styles, destroyed by marauders, the invaders of dreams and songs, are nourished by a heart swollen with visions.

The sweetish mixture in the peace-pipe at the dawn of illumination takes hold of all that surrounds our affection, stretching the horizons of our love, the caresses of words on friendship.

At The Star-port

I thought that in your absence we would walk around
in a mild January climate disguised in emotions of
May.

Geographical recollections, the regions of my heart
reach as far as the excited passageways . . .
Children . . . Lingalan banter . . . waves in the first
person plural, my sense in prison and our
radioactive exchanges swell up between us
in illicit reflections.

Violet distortions.

You walk and I come running
You soliloquize and I babble
You ponder and I squander my dreams at the
market of illusions.

Extracts From *A Poem Sequence*

She believes she hears a Creole cradlesong.
Capable at last of locating the pyromanic desire that
echoes in desolate, abandoned hotels, the fire
simmers, takes hold of the body in the unexpected
where the future sets fire to everything

*

A king of spades turns aside the ridicule of roguish
skylights, inviting them to foolishness.
My hands, pulling the shirt from his back, despair of
taking up our synchronized conversation again.
He speaks in a refrain, in erotic candour, poetry rising
far from ghostly and suspect intruders.
Shattering my blindness, setting free my muzzled
notions, his carefree glance lights up the table where I
stay seated the wrong way around in the tracks left by
powerful motorcycles.

Somehow, they always incarnate a restless and undying
passion that I recognize.
With bit in teeth, their galactic convoy catapults me
into rushing dustclouds that break every speed limit.

*

Strait-jacketed, an aerial view, taken during the aquatic
ballet, glides into the fragile tempest of waters.
An ingratiating darkness sleeps, nylon-stockinged up
to its neck.
Morose, incubating grotesque strides, it distorts the
season with its squalls.

But my handsome Apache, even riddled with despair
your charm feeds the drumming of our hearts.
Aimed like a phallic symbol, playing in aphrodisiacal
dimensions, your sweep swings toward an imagined
west where we take ourselves for important personages.

Distracted now, I forget our conversations on the
station benches where the flies seize upon very little.

DANIEL DUGAS

Daniel Dugas was born in Montréal in 1959. He is a visual artist and
musician, whose multimedia performance pieces, called "cubes-per-
formances," have toured Canada.

Publications: *L'Hara-Kiri de Santa-Gougouna* (Éditions Perce-
Neige, 1983), *Les Bibelots de tungstène* (Michel Henry Éditeur, 1989).

Michelin

black innards
that we took and blew up
to go out onto the sea
the guts or those buoys

which kept us from drowning
trailed behind us
like flying cannonballs
like chinaware gods
to keep us from dying
to keep us from fleeing
the smell of dead rays
that rose and fell on the beach like dead women
to keep us from opening our hands
and looking at our lifelines
to find out whether it's yes or no
whether we will still be alive tomorrow

black innards

blown-up inners

blown-up innards

that we grip again to remind us
of vacations in 1963
and the carefree beaches of Caraquet
black innards saved only in the deadmen of midnight
   bathing
still caress our thighs
and steal from us once more the blue of our hands

The Red Scarf

it was Summer in the suburbs
it was Summer almost agonizingly so
a man arrived
a man by himself tall with a red scarf on his neck
and from the depth of the suburb
as if suburbs could have depth
a child came up on his tricycle
crying out in the Summer silence
believing in eternal holidays while tearing up holidays
he came near the man and questioned him

the child "why have you got a red scarf on your
    neck?"
the man "I don't know"
the child "are you a communist?"
and the man replied "perhaps I don't know"

with these words the child left on his tricycle
and the tatters of Summer trailed behind him,
like the flags of empires
perhaps he was going to tell his friends about the
    extraordinary adventure
that had happened to him
and the man dreamily fingering his red scarf
in the middle of suburbs where Summer was no
    longer itself
murmured "shit I thought I had put on my blue
    scarf"

In The Star-heap Over Our Heads

You had to choose what no longer existed
a bad gift more than a bad memory
you chose badly
you will have to leave now

I was in a room the other day
there was a record playing
and I was watching a picture on television
the picture did not go with the music
and I wanted to cry
and I turned my head
towards the outdoors
it was windy
and the leaves in the trees
were like hands waving *bye bye*
and the leaves did not go
with the music either
and I cried
quietly
shutting my eyes as tight as I could

here there was no war
people died from natural causes
and talked about ridiculous things

every day I went out into the street and it was worse
than going to war
we ourselves were the ridiculous things
who marched off without saying good-day
who stared at the toes of our shoes
as if they were capes of sand
and were going to come apart
when the tides came back from having conquered
    the capes
on the other side of the world

here there was no war
people died from natural causes
and talked about ridiculous things

and I recall
we had oily hair
we had oily skin
and our souls, too, were getting oily
and god would no longer want us
we who dreamed of organized voyages
when down there end-of-the-world voyages were
    organized

here there was no war
people died from natural causes
and talked about ridiculous things

I left the houses
like atomic bomb shelters
my neighbours were in diving suits
we held out our hands
in the greenish skies
and we did not know the children's names
nor the colours of their eyes
so thick was the glass in our diving suits

there was no war here
only a little bit of hate
there was no war here
only ridiculous people
who dreamed of a great war
who dreamed of not dying
who dreamed of loving one day
there never had been war here
just a little bit of hate

out of long assurances
the solitary dogs
are baying, livid
in the dark
like coyotes
without a pack, alone
on the beach of bathers
seeking shade like love
and the terns are crying
as they wheel, white overhead
their shit will go
to dirty the salt sea,
their eyes as well
rubbing against the sunlight
on the grey sand
in the stormy gales
of the hearts' storms

on the dying waves
algae die too,
drying up on the coast
like green corpses

and the seashells
and agates
lost amid the nights of black waters
among moons drowned in salt crystals
and iodine breezes
and the great gusts that sweep
day and night

like silver lightning
making us see the ocean
and count each wave
without taking in the whole ocean any more

on the beach
the bathers
protest strongly
at dying like seaweed
with their parasols against the rain
and the sound of the sea
against missing looks
against my look sometimes
and yours, too,
at the horizon

under the tides
boats
men
under the sterns
in the view of human bathers
those who eat up emptiness
as one eats an animal
with blood in its veins
with a soul at its core
and eyes for its orbits
under the tides:
out of marine depths
and eyes at midday
those who watch from the beach
toward hallucinative solitudes
far off, over there

under the tides
at each hour
under a ton of water
luminous fish
swim in the shadows
knowing nothing
neither of those bathing

nor of those making love
nor of the sun that is shining
for a few meters of life

And then finally I have
only the palms of my hands
like future promises
the lines inside the palms
like agates inside the sea

the winds have ceased
Happiness is in me
like great sayings

gulls are flying above the strand

it is late in the world
you take in the street corners on two irises
it is late in our hearts
and some are throwing up here and there
it is late
it is late late
and your irises
are galloping like Mongols in flooding wastelands

in the winds the other day
I saw kites
flying
so high
that the kites were gods
and if they would return to earth
we would embrace them
to bid them welcome

and loftier still among
half-dead clouds
a D.C. 9 that awakened me

CALIXTE DUGUAY

A well-known musician and composer, with several recordings to his credit, Calixte Duguay was born in Saint-Marie-sur-Mer on the island of Lamèque in 1939. In 1974 he won the Grand Prix de la chanson du Festival de Granby. He has performed in Canada, the United States and Europe.

Publications: *Les Stigmates du silence* (Éditions d'Acadie, 1975).

To Marie

Forgive me, Marie
If I talk to you of seashells
White pebbles and white sand
If my words of love
Filtered in the nets of rage
Allow only the effluvia
Of wind-foam and sea-winds to pass
And let a few gulls
And a few seabirds
Come to whirl round and round there.

I have nothing else to offer you
Marie
I from a land without cathedrals
From a town without mysteries
From a house where apparitions
Have long ago
Ended their rendez-vous.

The goldsmiths who cut this hard diamond
Worked hard at it with a file
Hanging on only with docile and muted patience
I keep in my heart a great despair
That has not yet been put to sleep
By little jigging tunes
Of the violins of time
And of people.

Meanwhile
Marie
Come tell me that it feels good
To breathe in the day's bloom
And the vast fields of purple clover
And our mornings white with ice frost and snow
As I hold onto hope
In this great pity I feel
For the people of my homeland.

To Have A Homeland

To say, My Acadie
As they say, My China
As they will say one day
Maybe,
My *Kébek*
And to feel in your womb
A quivering
Like hunger for bread from home
And the thrill of belonging

To have your eyes wide open
As if to catch the messages
Of its trees and flowers
Of air fire salt and water

To clench in your fists the gravel
Of the road that leads
To the top of the orchard
While languidly dragging
Your feet
Over a bridge with handrails
On the road to Philorome

To want to cover up with the sand
Of an old world
The mechanized springs
Of telephones
And motor-horns

To call out to your Acadian woman
Because you want her to love
The words of an archaic speech
Brought up to date
For the staging of a new kind of play

To caress the hair of our very own women

To trace with fingers the onslaught
Of thousands of sunbeams on their bare bodies
Golden as hay in the month of June

To shake the hand of a Cap-Pelé fisherman
On the waste of our fallow fields

To dig in the north of Miscou Island
The trenches of our hopes

To look there for our treasure island

To get your toes wet
In the green water of the Restigouche

That is what is meant by having a homeland

The Stigmata Of Silence

The stigmata of silence
Have too long bruised our hands
And our feet
Which can walk no longer
In this land of solitude
And sea and soil

When he will come this Redeemer
To save our own little world
Of yesterday today and tomorrow
Especially our own little world of tomorrow
Washing away in torrents
Two centuries of refined patience

And cryptic words
And the hewing of wood
And the drawing of water
For others from the wells of others
Shall we know how to recognize him
This Christ of renewal
Before he is placed on the cross
Or must he burst forth
As far as the words themselves
In cries of crimes and retributions
So that our numb skinny fingers
May begin to spark the flame
Like streamlined locomotives
Launched at top speed

And you, bare-breasted woman
Shuddering
Your sex unveiled
To give birth to a cry
Which puts freedom on street corners
Within range of your voice
Will you be only an ornament of a whore-house?

O stigmata of silence
I feel you in me
Like a blade of fear
Thrust
Into the guts of centuries
And the flank of my own people

May once and for all
The silver-voiced, steel-tongued Conqueror
Come if it is possible
To sound the awakening reveille
On a morning luminous like no other
May the drum with bloody skin
Beaten to a pulp
Knock out crazy rhythms on my country's roads
Or else it will soon be over
May a funeral hearse come and drop us

By the same roads
Like stinking filth
Into the gully of oblivion

GÉRARD ÉTIENNE

Born in Haiti in 1936, Gérard Étienne has lived for many years in Moncton, where he is a Professor of linguistics and journalism at the Université de Moncton. He has written many editorials and articles in newspapers, magazines and scholarly journals. His work has been translated into English, Portugese and German.

Publications: Poetry: *Au Milieu des larmes* (Togiram Press, 1960), *Plus large qu'un rêve* (Éditions Dorsainville, 1960), *La Raison et mon amour* (Les Presses Port-au-princiennes, 1961), *Gladys* (Éditions Panorama, 1963), *Lettre à Montréal* (Éditions L'Estérel, 1966), *Dialogue avec mon ombre* (Éditions francophones du Canada, 1972), *Cri pour ne pas crever de honte* (Nouvelle Optique, 1982).

Fiction: *Le Nègre crucifié* (Éditions Nouvelle Optique, 1974; new edition: Éditions Metropolis, 1989), *Un Ambassadeur macoute à Montréal* (Éditions Nouvelle Optique, 1980), *Une Femme muette* (Éditions Nouvelle Optique, 1983), *La Reine Soleil levée* (Éditions Guérin, 1987, new edition: Éditions Metropolis, 1989).

Ah My Love Flutters . . .

Ah my love flutters lighter than a bird-poem
and places sparkling feet on my hope grown tall with
                                                           darkness
This great weakness love tells of
Immense bogs painted with sun-rays
That long rope wrapping up human matter
the might of minerals and the heat of seasons
that flame of fire in the flesh of space like a beak or
                                                           a kiss
ripe fruit fleeing in the maiden dew
Oh it assumes the headaches of my piled-up loves
it assumes the reason for writing down all my loves

it warms beneath my palms this winter of
                                        tenderness
this piece of my heart broken like a crystal
But if for a little of you in my reveries
                                        metamorphoses
I sing you, a half-moon in myself and my torments
they will say that I sin against the strength that is
    your strength
they will say that my whole self is soft velvet in its
    folly
they will say that the sky is too light for my head
they will say who knows what
that your image dissolves in fog
and evaporates in sobbing vapours

There are oceans between our dreams and me
the world runs at my feet fresher than desire for
                                        women
and in the evening's turbulence
as in the swift flight of crickets
I hold time in my hand
I squeeze time like a ripe fruit in the breeze
                                        make love
time my poem that I love and that nurses me
my gluttony my driving force and my knowledge
reality
time that good fellow in my friend's eye
that mechanical thrust that makes my heart wander
through the too-frail waves of my desire

My love you are everything to me
you are the cry of Marie-Jude, my tenth sun
you are the sweet confession of Gladys
dewdrops of dawn in the indentation of leaves
my nourishment my eucharist my arteries my black
    nights
My love you are everything to me
slumber with its ample setting
a gaze silvered with sobs and inhuman farewells
the morning star which twinkles in my breath
life in its new suit

My love you are everything
the lynched dream of my fallen comrade in prison
manhood's kingdom coming open in the morning like a
                                                    petal

THE PEOPLE and their little hills of hope

My love you are everything
You are like Port-au-Prince in its frenzy
inside my room you take the form of Cuba
seeking Marti's voice
you are the heart of Africa, tom-toming the world in
                                        its deep forests
You are Spain in my burning fever
those suns of Chile beyond my awaking

but why my love this dance so frail
in verse so poor from a poet
why all these gleanings in the field of my
                                        inspirations
when their hands bring weeping
from the whip
from defiling
from lynching
from tearing to pieces

when they put a stop to children dancing in the
    moonlight
and break down doors and eat at reason

Of what use is love if it is not for loving

Of what use is love
if it is not for watering sorrow and grief

Of what use is love
if it is not for making heart-stalks bloom

Of what use is love
if it is not to join a great *coumbite*
of reunited days and nights

Listen my love
the season of love comes quickly
it runs away quickly and hurries up the time for
    loving
it clangs loud, the bell of love

Listen
evening enters your hair my love
hears the fierce shout from the *springfields* over there
that uproots your love my love
listen my love
the earth trembles at the approach of love
the hurrahs and applauses of the harvesters of love
O my love dialectic of the hymns of love
everything that is of you is me and us
they want to break you down as one breaks down a
    stare
they want to uproot you as one uproots from the sky a

                                      star

you power and strength
God and demon
mountains and oceans
words and truths
illuminations and their opposites

My love leave my love
straighten your spine to heights loftier than reason
and pursue your course
in our flower beds of innocence and peace
for the great weeding-out of invented agonies

Be the wrath of a river
become my folly my form
my courage my light
For the happiness of nations I want to pile up suns
and want you my love to flutter like a dream
to lay yourself soundlessly on the layers of the world
where you will open with your hands of steel and
    flesh
The sluice gates of peace.

It Is Snowing Outside...

It is snowing outside. Haitian slaves chained up in the Dominican Republic are coming into my room again. In their loose-fitting jackets they comprise dozens of skeletons. Haitian refugees are re-entering my grief as well. They have broken teeth, arms cut up; they wear their guts in their hair. Their laments reach the ceiling and their stinking sweat falls back on the growing helplessness of my face.

Out of that group of dead flesh invading my room, an old Negress stands out. Daylight narrows slowly in her eyes as the Chief's dragoons plunge their daggers into the breast of Jacques Stephen Alexis, the revolutionary. She refuses to hand over her system, that starveling stomach out of which pours caterpillers thirsting for blood.

I bear witness to an old dewdrop shaker. He dances around a coffin; his tones are snapped out as if his voice, beaten by ants and wasps, were going to make the timbers of the house collapse. Then once more I vomit my lack of power. Slaves and refugees bring me back to my negro intellectual shabbiness, to all the principles which make me a verbal magician caught in a trap of words.
but I scream
but I suffer
and poverty
and crime
both make your brains pop
love, too,
the illusion of believing
that you are useful for something in this corner of
    the globe
for they make you walk in shame
all those words
for the king's daughter's rose garden
all those words
for the voodoo spirits of the President

So it is snowing outside
they are in my room
monsters created by men
And monsters
have devoured my people my face
They have uprooted my soul
which walked beside a beggar-woman
They have swallowed up the mornings
no upside-down stories
and they have knocked on my bedroom door
until the curtain was lowered
on the monster comedy

It is snowing outside
You know very well, Dominique,
that the dream of the great evening has sprouted
that our lantern in the streets
the vermin of verminous quarters
the antennae-wearing centipedes
have cut off the current that feeds the power

You know very well that this boat will not leave
The ones who should go are waiting
grill in hand
to greet the poet's prophecy

It is snowing
A new stomach cramp
makes me clench my teeth
my cage is revolting
that niece who has just landed in Moncton
skin and bones
with nothing to restore the reality
watered down by contradictions of the spirit
and in those wells of the dead
where the General's Saints go to be born again

It is snowing outside
my cage closes again
heavy and without regret

LÉONARD FOREST

Born in 1928 in Chelsea, Massachussets, Léonard Forest spent his childhood in Moncton before moving to Montréal, where he worked at the National Film Board and made a number of films on Acadie including *Pêcheurs de Pomcoup* and *Les Acadiens de la dispersion.* He was awarded the Prix France-Acadie in 1980 for *Comme en Florence,* his second collection of poetry, and has been a Canada Council grant recipient. He recently returned to live in Moncton.

Publications: *Saisons antérieures* (Éditions d'Acadie, 1973), *Comme en Florence* (Éditions d'Acadie, 1979).

Former Seasons

I

my seabirds inscribe me in enormous circles
    above the wharves of my connected summers.
my time draws itself out. I survey the shores of
    my former dreams. I sleep.
my solitudes plough the distant waters, they will
    come back to me full.

my summers are swollen with sunlight, they make
    and unmake themselves like fertile tides,
my absent days bloom with women's names,
I summon them to the calm and permanent
    weddings of a time of reconciliation.
my boats, too, are well-known to me. reassured, I
    rhyme off their double first names. I have not
    forgotten them.
my seabirds inscribe very slowly the curves of my
    enormous bright lassitude.

II

we shall not go into the city. autumn
    will come without surprising us.

by day our boats will carry back the sea winds,
    and we shall recognize them.
by night the souls of our dead will not cease
    their whistling at our windows,
we shall recognize them, together we shall say
    the rosaries of their innumerable
    names, we shall invite them to be among
    our everyday family.
they will be silent. and we shall be cradled in
    the vast and motionless kitchen
    of our belonging.
our weather will complain. the rain
    will splash our unsubdued mourning. the wrong
    side of the weather will summon us
    like fiery boats.
we shall face the wind out to the farthest tip of
    the wharf. we shall stay there.
for shelter we have only the shelter of our
    dead. autumn will pass
    without wounding us.
we shall not go into the city.

III

I have winters that rock like moored boats.
I say nothing. a woman sings from
    one day to the next the high tide of her
    fullness.
my voices are soft and far off.
    my past dwells under
    the same roof.
I hear a fraternal voice where the child
    of my children gambles with
    the oldest of memories.
my expectations are yesterday's songs. my
    nostalgia weaves white expanses
    of hope.
winter. my boats are motionless. winter
    freezes all journeys. winter confines.
winter is everything we are.

winter is innocent joy. winter is
  a gull arrested on the wing,
winter is with us like a holiday we have expected.
we listen to ourselves. my dreams make themselves
    at home in the warmth of winter like a boat
    in the water.
my winters possess me and give me notice.
I listen.

IV

wasn't it always the saturday before easter that
    the ice broke up in the bay.
wasn't it always at three o'clock on the friday
    of jesus christ
that a soft sadness lit up our feelings
    of complicity.
wasn't it always the daylight of that glorious
    sunday,
at the hour of innocent vespers,
that a new vigour sounded the celebration in the
    back-country,
the terrestrial harbour of our maritime homeland.
is it not from the depth of our most powerful
    recollections,
is it not from the depth of our everlasting good-byes,
is it not from the depth of our mourning, from the
    depth of our wanderings, from the depth of our
    aching patrimony,
is it not from the depth of a nostalgic and fraternal
    destiny
that our summer will be born.

And I Dreamed Of A Great Black Sun

I

the sound is sounded
the belfry bells toll hopelessly

and on the pavement
it rains.

horseshoes have passed
over the pavement
and wheels have turned
as a millstone turns.
a dead man in his box sleeps
more deeply
while the bells let their sad sobs fall
    onto the wet
pavement.

and the tiny widow at the back
is blacker than the night,
her little feet go squeak squeak in the water
while her dead man sleeps,
the bells rain down
and her dampened heart
goes flip flop under the millstone wheel
that eight horseshoes draw
over the pavement where it rains.

II

the dead were not there
not even in spirit
nor in body
naturally
the dead were not there
because they were dead.
the dead were not there
because they love neither war
nor memories of war
nor talk about it
nor timed silences
nor funeral processions
because they are dead men
quite simply
and because they no longer have feelings

these dead men
neither for nor against
neither the war
nor the peace
which we could let them have.

III

the pope is dead
the king is dead
the school master has swallowed poison
I no longer have king
nor master
nor holy father to rule over me.
the queen is dead with her king
the pope is dead his dogma as well
and the little school mistress no longer teaches
　　anything but love.
I no longer have law
nor fear, nor restraint
nor sorrow.
I reign.

IV

You know what they have done.
You know,
pale, at the end of the garden, the bust
　　of Homer.
they have killed Homer.

Remember at Chartres
the blue fire of stained glass,
sacred.
They have put out the fire of Chartres.

Chartres,
　　Homer,
　　　　Phaedra . . .

Phaedra, you recall, wept her elegant grief aloud
And as a play replayed every night, her classic plight
Stirred up the passions of a crowd infatuated
By this tearful mistress. Phaedra is silent tonight.

They have killed Phaedra.

V

we shall go into the city
we shall walk the length
    of lost wharves
and say nothing.
we shall go into the city
that is dead
and we shall play at death
which is nothing.
we shall go into the city
and we will love
along the wharves
along the streets
without laughter or tears
for this city is dead
but death is nothing.

VI

Do not mourn the deaths to come,
    nor the coming on of your own funeral.
You will not die at all, nor will
    your children.
You will not leave orphans behind.

They will not touch the children at play
Nor the pregnant women. Nor the old, either,
Who sleep wide-eyed
Nor the infirm, nor the sick
    in the dry depths of their insomnia.

They will touch nothing, but everything will stop.
And no one will remember anything any more,
neither grief nor children nor dead men
in the dry depths of non-being.

No one will be touched.
Snow-white death will fall like a blessing
and we shall no longer be anything in its
    large and luminous open hand.
You will see,
light will empty itself in a single blaze
and we shall get a good night's sleep at last.

My Royal Roads

how easy it is to love love,
opening secret doors once again
and lighting tall candles
from an ancient Easter
suspended on the threshold of one's self.
my royal roads are long and straight,
my heart runs along them and does not come back.

how easy it is to love love,
the lip that drinks the pulp
of originality, the eye that examines
the restless land of a celebration
open into the shadows of memory.

my royal roads are long and straight,
my heart runs along them and does not come back.

how easy it is to love love,
and every time repeat
its perfection: to sing in two voices
hearing the joy to be had
out of a most enduring love.

my royal roads are long and straight,
my heart runs along them and does not come back.

how easy it is to love love,
to give up the heart's hand
under the warm sands of a dream,
building in its spanish castles
only simple tragic celebrations.

my royal roads are long and straight,
my heart runs along them and does not come back.

how easy it is to love love,
to live in it always at a distance,
sometimes picking up its lost thread
like a song in the habit
of crying at time's convenience.

my royal roads are long and straight,
my heart runs along them without coming back.

Itineraries

you imagine me aspiring to rhyme,
already drunk with shocking words that ring
at the end of lines whose loud thunders bring
both the proof and the brilliance of the crime.

to you the dream I have appears to be,
among shy ravings, a stage-managed plan:
in this my sin is but little better than
the love of gold or punctuality.

I confess to you that you will not find
my path like that of any official,
and that I do not know the hour at all
in which daydreams are normally confined.

I drop my less-wise beasts into the black
abyssmal depths of my nights' dark shadow,
I stir their hunger, I do not allow
them to bring me any good tidings back.

I do not know what nightmare entertainment
from such perfect rhymes as mine will befall,
nor do I know what frightful festival
from the depths of this mind-pool will be sent.

My nocturnal poise scorns the precision
of prose in this case; it desires verse
to be its medium, this thing perverse
that cites as authority derision.

just as one sows seeds I plant poetry,
I know all its beginnings well enough,
what I'll never know is what kind of stuff
will spring up from that madness in me.

my rapture owes nothing to wine at all,
although it may happen, I must confess,
that I go to it to ease my distress,
but, Lord! never in vain on it do I call!

MELVIN GALLANT

Born in Urbainville, Prince Edward Island in 1932, Melvin Gallant received his doctorate from the Université de Neuchâtel and has been a professor of literature at the Université de Moncton since 1964. He received the Prix France Acadie for his novel *Le Chant des grenouilles* in 1983.

Publications: Poetry: *L'Été insulaire* (Éditions d'Acadie, 1982).

Fiction: *Ti-Jean, contes acadiens* (Éditions d'Acadie, 1973), *Caprice à la campagne* (Éditions d'Acadie, 1982), *Le chant des grenouilles* (Éditions d'Acadie, 1982), *Caprice en hiver* (Éditions d'Acadie, 1984).

Essays and Non-Fiction: *La Cuisine traditionnelle en Acadie* (with Marielle Boudreau, Éditions d'Acadie, 1973), *Guide de la cuisine traditionnelle acadienne* (with Marielle Boudreau, Éditions Stanké, 1980), *Le Pays d'Acadie* (Éditions d'Acadie, 1982; trans. by Elliot Shek, *The Country of Acadia*, Simon & Pierre, 1986), *Portraits d'écrivains* (with Ginette Gould, Éditions d'Acadie, 1982).

Extracts From *An Island Summer*

1

I come through the garden door
and I still hear the sound of your laughter
bouncing off the wall
a laugh
abrupt, sparkling and playful
always ending like a wave
losing itself among the pebbles on the beach
the same laugh
the same sound
the same movement
as when we played
under the olive trees
and you hid behind every tree
calling in a mocking tone
I'm the sparrow you dream about

the sun drenched your hair with light
giving it silvered highlights
to the sea's applause
and the dazzling charm
of five thousand years of light and love
seeped slowly into my heart

21

peaceful
the old Mikonian women sit
breathing the softness of the night
their greetings are affectionate and wordy
they always have something to talk about
children growing tall
life slipping by
the world changing
people they have known
and loved

and who have gone
forever

from time to time one leaves her bench
to go into a church
to light a few tapers
or burn incense there

the shadow still stands out
against the whiteness of the walls
even late at night
under the amused eye of the moon
and the narrow streets seem to open their arms
to the light as to the passers-by

you greeted me
a stranger in this world
gave me bread and wine
and made me share
the light and love of your people

your gentle mockery
still lives in my memory
the houses of Mikonos are so white, you assert
because Nicholas spills the flour
that takes flight on the wind
and settles on all the houses

they are now like great white gulls
streaking the blue sky
above our mingled bodies

it was too soon for you to leave
you should have warned me
prepared me for it
let me hibernate in you
and you in me

come back
I want to watch the sun passing
in the depths of your eyes

for as long as a song lasts
come back
I want to breathe in once more
the salt scent of your hair
in the mildness of a warm evening
come back
I want just to look at you
to hear you speak
and tell you
sweet and tender things

34

I still hear your voice
breaking into a song
whose whole meaning I now understand

an mai agapois ké ine oniro
pote na mi xipniso...

words that go straight to my heart
like a calvalcade on the road
in the middle of a downpour

why did you have to leave without warning
why did I have to believe your story
of going for coffee at Melina's
a breach of trust
an unforgiveable betrayal

that evening
I thought I would die
I could no longer catch my breath
my heart was jammed
in the jaws of a vice
my hands were trembling
and my head wanted to split open

38

In vain I hold back my memory
urging it to move into its back room
that story of a time gone by
images rise up again
one after another
to the surface
like the coolness of a spring
in the middle of this arid land

yesterday still
you rode down
the wild, dry slopes of Tourlos
before me on a donkey
to pick ripe grapes
in the Alkis vineyards
today
joking with the waiter at the café
who could not find our bill
you said that perhaps we were only an illusion
and had never eaten there

Anna Vera
I learned so many things beside you
to listen better to the sound of a voice
hear better the harmony of noises
look around me
seize upon the meaning of a simple gesture
distinguish beauty
in the movements of a dance
know the price of freedom
discover a people's soul
taste the delights
of knowing the other
allowing myself to be overcome by it
wanting to halt time
so that one single instant
might become
eternity

39

writing is a gesture of absence

ULYSSE LANDRY

A musician, composer and writer, Ulysse Landry has composed music for several films including Claude Renaud's 1979 film, *Souvenirs d'un écolier,* and Herménégilde Chiasson's 1985 film, *Toutes les photos finissent par se ressembler.* Born in Cap Pelé, New Brunswick in 1950, his writing has been presented in performance and appeared in various periodicals.

Publications: *Tabous aux épines de sang* (Éditions d'Acadie, 1977).

And This Program . . .

And this program that you watch on T.V.
is not finished
between a soap so gentle
and an orgasmic toothpaste
  SEX-APPEAL
you will replay the lives of others

While in silence
  they fiddle with the handcuffs
  those they assassinate for real don't make the news
  and the battles which will never have names
  remain silent
  to the sound of the trumpet
  on orders of the administration
  an immense billboard is enough
  the blasphemous phallus of our everyday death
AFTER ALL SHE'S GOT THE FRESHEST MOUTH IN TOWN
and the silence hardly matters
to those for whom noise no longer has ears

We will replay the lives of others

on a 22-inch screen
   in fibreglass colours
We will replay the lives of others
   at set times
   between other times deathly heavy
instead of confessing the lie
   which steals away our nights
   under the plastic eyes of fear
We will replay the lives of others
inventions of a thousand dizzy spells
   our swollen sexes
   live apart in preserved orgasms
   and we learn to make love standing up
   between a box of *SPIC AND SPAN*
   and a can of *PEPSI*
   FOR THOSE WHO THINK YOUNG

And our 22-inch screens
in fibreglass colours
have lost the shape of those faces
that I embraced in the half-light of anxiety
have lost the shape of that refrain
that at dusk you sang to me
to send away all those electronic ghosts

But we will replay the lives of others
and our songs in collective stereo
will wear themselves out in mummified juke boxes

Yes we will replay the lives of others
   between a hamburger and *a french fried*
To die of our own death

Screaming Against Tomorrow's Silence

I

A lengthy pause on the world's summit
stops us from moving beyond

since two-headed serpents
disguised as swallows
are patrolling the valley of the jesting gods

it has been centuries since the moon was seen
going down on the dim horizon

my mother was a whore in former times
and I went across a land
where the ocean stroked my feet
and made fun of me

since then the sea has shifted colours
and our islands have slid
under the weight of silver skyscrapers

that is why
I sell hard times
    on squalid street corners
    at the fag-end of a dying nation
I sell hard times
    on the frontiers of slums
    or else

    on the plundered symbol of all our famines
    hidden inside the uncommitted jewel box of
    our forgotten geographies

between two forests
with their trees of steel
I hide under a name found by chance
and I sell hard times
    coloured like entrails flayed
    by all our premature abortions
    coloured like sun-dried skulls
    to frighten children
    to torment toads
    or perhaps even
    for lack of anything better
    to ape the dreams of our jailers

once upon a time we learned
to play soldier in our Sunday clothes
and between family rosaries
we cursed and swore in English
because of a thousand meaningless glances
that held us responsible for the virtue of fools
and so that we might not die condemned
we collected our stations of the cross
and we made love
hiding our sex beneath woollen mittens

since then, the cemeteries have grown
thanks to our damned trouble
and on the battlefields where we died
they have sown commas between the lines
to confuse the tourists

II

The hard times that I sell
have the taste of sin and the colour of death
sometimes weary from my too regular masturbation
I piss with tenderness on the photo of my first
    communion
and hook an obscene lantern onto our lies

bored with selling my hard times
and screaming against tomorrow's silence
I plan complicated new systems
for rediscovering our engulfed frontiers
for rediscovering our faces
in an outpouring of speech
in the simplified words of love

the lightening flash of my joys
shattered against a wall of ignorance

is it a matter of opening just one eye
or of multiplying glances

so as not to have to regret too bitterly
the naivety we have had
kneeling
while waiting for the hour of the angelus

let us pause a little to think
of the slaps in our faces
the unrestrained caresses whose treason we stumbled
　　upon
or else
like tomorrow's rubbish
we shall return to our slums again

III

Oh you know
all the time I've spent
giving you advice
I could very well have spent changing
the position of the garbage cans in our heads
all you have to do is think about it
to find once more the origin of our misfortunes

Too often we have talked about
our ancestral war
Too often we have mentioned
the exploits of our fathers
Too long we have mourned
the woes of history

but nevertheless
despite the high priests of our shame
we insist on dying
martyrs
of our dreams
and condemned to hunger
we await the rifle shots
with children's hands
and frogs' heads
and tomorrow will come later than yesterday

breathless from the long road
it has travelled for no reason at all

I could write of other martyrs
on velour paper
and sing with guitars larger than life
but
I keep still
in order to hear my heart's awakening
in ardent gasps
and I await the orgies of love
in order to recover from our death

however
it snows showers
in the dandelion fields of our *backyard tableau*
and the country which owned miracles in its name
has played too strongly against the howling wind
for we have always been flapping in the north wind
on clotheslines too short because of poverty
and later still we shall float half-naked
in the barrels of salted herring
under the screams of gulls and wounded seabirds
screams of death
screams of forgetting
anticipation is blocked
awakening is extinguished
on the future's rusty nail

misery
how cold am I from all this stillness
misery
how hard it is
to learn to talk out loud

JEANNINE LANDRY-THÉRIAULT

Jeannine Landry-Thériault, winner of the Prix France-Acadie for her first novel, *Un soleil mauve sur la baie,* is a full-time writer. She was born in 1937 in St-Paul de Grande-Anse, New Brunswick.

Publications: Fiction: *Un soleil mauve sur la baie, Tome 1* (Éditions d'Acadie, 1981), *Le Moustiquaire, Tome 2* (Éditions d'Acadie, 1982).

Non-Fiction: *La Vie au bout des doigts* (biography, Éditions du Fleuve, 1987).

Femmenolence

Love dies in a crash of slippery ice. The thunder of its directions scatters like star-dust. Its desire evaporates like a funeral notice: its imagined lover crumbled on the fairness of a freshly washed floor. The mirror is broken: seven years of bad luck . . .

The woman recedes, loses herself in a flash of perpetual somnolence.

A little girl with straight braids facing the convent and the blood: virgin, spouse, devoted mother . . . Fan of tears, of full breasts. Indistinct shapes: sucking it in from inside . . . disorganized, eccentric.

The sunshine sneaks in, in a filigree on her beginning-to-blush skin beginning to sweat with those regrets which fade under the cruel mantle of the menopause . . . Soon it will be said behind her back: "She was beautiful, she was young, she was . . . "

Sterile in body and ideas, fertile in offspring, slattern, high-spirited, nice, promiscuous, marginal, mediocre . . . Terms of the masters, nicknames or descriptions? They remember, my aunts do . . . Their fair skin, their red hair, their legs hidden beneath the eiderdown. What if she dared, the woman with blueberry eyes: what if she began to cry, to let go, to dance in her summer kitchen . . .

The grandfather clock would suddenly find its workings paralysed. Time suspended like a bell . . . If she dared, the woman with hair of ebony, her skin aflower with rage under a white apron . . . The man came in, weary from his daily toil . . . white shirt crumpled . . . The brunette did not budge. Her apron was curled up, her knees wobbled . . . Her hair, tied in a bun, fell like a forgotten bridal veil . . . black like the open hole of the mirror . . . The man, dazzled and immune from maternity, wanted to be avenged for his day's work . . . The brunette escaped into quicksilver . . . She dared, the woman with the blueberry eyes dared . . . She said: "No!"

Earlier Seasons

The townspeople brought in their luggage, the acrid smells of crumpled leather, of the bottled fragrance "Midnight in Paris."
My room suddenly changed its aspect, its face . . . Immediately were erased the odour of beeswax, of my mother's sweet-smelling bread, of toilet-soap soaked in lavender . . .
The lilac blossoms blushed with envy, surrounded by plastic bric-à-brac . . . Summer at Bois Tranquille was suffocating, filtering in everywhere like thieves disguised as vacationers, cousins from the States arriving, bullying, ironic, Americanized . . .

White Easter shoes were brought down from the attic, yawning, in their cardboard boxes . . . The poplars and the cherry trees green at last . . . Coupling on the yellow grass reserved for woolly caterpillars, future innocent butterflies . . .
Azure sea, August 15 matins; ancestral turquoises; washed-out colours of a restored flag.
Red, like apples "borrowed" from Thaddeus's orchard, the September sunsets blush for the sins of Summer . . .
Sprigs of fragrant hay tickling my virgin thighs in

anticipation . . . Linen dried under hidden looms . . .
White have become the black locks of the sweating
woodcutters . . .
Papa died on Epiphany. The sentinel icicles melted
beneath the eaves; you might say, July in January . . .
White have remained mamma's handkerchiefs.
Green are my confused thoughts in the Autumn of my
life . . .
Rose, scarcely touched, my imaginary romances . . .

GÉRALD LEBLANC

Born in Bouctouche in 1945, Gérald Leblanc received his education
from one year at university and his many travels. Among the most pro-
lific of Acadie's writers, his work has been published in Québec,
France, Belgium and Mexico.

Publications: *Comme un otage du quotidien* (Éditions Perce-Neige,
1981), *Géographie de la nuit rouge* (Éditions d'Acadie, 1984), *Précis
d'intensité* (with Herménégilde Chiasson, *Lèvres urbaines* #12, 1985),
Lieux transitoires (Michel Henry Éditeur, 1986), *L'Extrême frontière,
poèmes 1972-1988* (Éditions d'Acadie, 1988).

Architect Of The Feast

on flimsy ground
your motions embrace
the surrounding space.
I call these motions: dance,
and I call for the choreographer.
around the table, we have drunk colours
I am learning structures and dimensions
the wind in your hair
without my glasses
there are your hands
and the gentle geometry of your body.

First Place

This language we are learning
in the folds of unmade beds
this language obedient to the blue impulses
plugged into our mouths
our hands our sex our thighs
our eyes make contact and quicken
to the very fibres of organic music
in a live essence
of breath the brain exudes
in chemical mornings
every ionized caress
I remember dreams are a river
flowing through on our networks
of awareness

we are attaining the memory of a first place
we are experiencing this state in our bodies
eaten up by pure energy
which has become current fold ember
of this language we are learning

Complicity

the taste of your skin sweating in the dance
among the graffiti and the oohooo from the bar
I taste your red anarchy
your movements translate our complicity
the mauve vibrations of our desire
I hear the night traffic
that new record which is playing everywhere
the cracking of preconceived notions
and you, too,
you hear it

Acadielove

i love you
and Bouctouche awakes in me
with my father's speech
(my country is a chain of villages
or a drunken jig or a clothesline)
i love you
in the dawn of images to be born
in a poem
at the bootlegger's
to the rhythms of a mad violin
on the road to Tracadie
in a field of clover
in the dirty streets of Moncton
you are there
and my roots are singing

To Love You

a covered bridge
as fine as Notre Dame
a lobster trap
the smell of tar on the wharf
I move through this between your hands
as true as your eyes tell
of a new world within your body
we are alike in our thirst
sometimes your laugh
reaches down to my guts
and my poems take form

January Stillness

love is a white space breathing in January stillness. in
a gripping silence. i meditate on its whiteness as i wait
for my desires to play themselves out.

to speak of love. that is to come back to words once again. *parlez-moi d'amour* like the song. once upon a time like in the stories. i notice that songs and stories are becoming mingled. i notice that i am going ahead blindly into something. i notice that i am opening my eyes. it is a story of here, a story with a local flavour, a sense of place.

the first time i saw love's face, i was burnt. the first burn made me look for fire in every face i met. i thought of the first fire, in the beginning.

love is a white space breathing in January stillness. in this whiteness i see pictures of you again. your words return in the stillness: "We shall see each other, we shall dream each other." i dream in your mouth, i dream in your body. because love looks like you. because *can, talmak, ulak.* because a current is passing. because the season goes forward. because the earth turns. because we are turning with it.

and the other side of love which is indifference and the upside down of love which is blackness. i invoke images of light to cross through all that. my favourite things: like Woody Allen in *Manhattan*, like Miles Davis' clear brass in *My Funny Valentine*, like Édith Piaf's rough voice in the immensity of desire, like Matisse's Studio, like Anne Waldman's hair, like Michael Delisle's *l'Extase neutre*, like Sharon Thesen's laughter, like Yolande's voice on the telephone, like your name breathing in January stillness.

i have felt you here in this world for some time. i was waiting patiently. and you are there at the rendez-vous. you are my ally in getting through reality. you know matter is a flexible illusion. you know we can join each other through thoughts. you know that space breathes in time. you know that words transmit energy, and you know that i love you.

i sit in a white room, in the city, some time in the 80's. a stucco wall produces moving patterns when i concentrate on it. i close my eyes. i breathe; i inhale, i exhale, i inhale, i exhale, *hamsa*. in a white room.

my body is a cat coiled on a mat. i stretch out and draw myself up, arching from my head and feet. my thighs are warming up and my sex is throbbing. i stretch out on my back. i breathe: i inhale, i exhale. hamsa.

i enter a hypnagogic state. i float. i see white, then blue. i see your eyes. and i see myself in front of you: San Francisco. we are sitting in the Foster Cafeteria and we are talking about Allen Ginsberg and Peter Orlovsky. we make a mutual promise of commitment: of sharing our bodies and our consciousness. of both of us working through our earthly impulses so that our souls might find each other in heaven together. we are saying yes and we are weeping with joy in this world's disorder.

i open my eyes in the white room. i write love is a white space breathing in January stillness. days turn like a many-coloured mandala upon a white ground. i say the flowing words, love amethyst gleaming electric, that ransack the senses. i say love your name an inviting image on the soundtrack of our explorations. i say love your name a mantra for stringing together the hours of daytime. i say love a timeless poem of delight, love hands, love eyes, love legs, love sex, love soul when all our fibres are shining in love birth. in the noonday of seizing passion. in the light framing us in the trajectory. in the white space breathing in January stillness.

Voices

the arguments I have in
my head with you or is it me

unendingly talking to myself
examining one option and its
opposite from which come these voices
that sometimes I call
poetry

MONIQUE LEBLANC

A television journalist with Radio-Canada and an actress, Monique Le-
blanc was born in Richibouctou, New Brunswick in 1960. She writes
poetry and plays including the screenplay for the film *Cap Lumière*.
   Publications: *Joanne d'où Laurence (ou le drame enregistré)* (Édi-
tions Perce-Neige, 1987).

End Of The Film

End of the film
so as not to become your screen
so as not to stick like a suction cup
in a lovesick way
I think of the plot I saw earlier

both plane and submarine
yellow-stamped and rouge-stained

I consider the plot I believed in earlier
its setting
circumflex between two lovers' heads
lower lips caffeinated
they are in their third sleepless night
their fourth delicious day
one a plane, the other a submarine
like the end of the film

credits to fit the occasion

Park Portugal
Far From The Mainland

Fifteen pigeons
for my fourteen minutes to waste
the random cooing
without pretence
of a tiny creature among so many others
and I think they are speaking to me

the young man as well
more ugly than handsome stretched out on a bench
watching and listening to
the old ladies who, like pages of a story,
with handbags, pass over feathers and duvets
remembering uncertain times

this is sublime speech and
a sign of affection
between bird and being
and I think they are speaking to me

RAYMOND GUY LEBLANC

One of Acadie's foremost poets, Raymond Guy LeBlanc was born in Moncton in 1945. A lecturer in Philosophy, LeBlanc is a PhD. candidate at the Université de Montréal. A musician and journalist, his poems and articles have been published in a number of periodicals and anthologies in Canada and Europe.

Publications: *Cri de terre (1969-71)* (Éditions d'Acadie, 1972; revised edition, 1986), *Chants d'amour et d'espoir* (Michel Henry Éditeur, 1988).

Flower

She is a prisoner of her shadow, and lost in it
Alternately awake and asleep

From the wind she knows the blossom-shift
A movement of earth's sap

She is a beam of rain
Cleansed on a stem that blooms forever

She is born of the twists of mysterious caverns
Where her perfume vanishes into thin air

From the day she knows a cloud in front of the sun
From the night a moon-leaf

She springs from life she springs from death
A broken harmony in our image

Winter

I knocked on your door with my injured hand
Winter having come into the human darkness

I knocked on your door with both hands
One already frozen and red from the crystal
    whiteness
Where the moon was setting

I knocked on your door with the breath of my
    mouth
But that breath got caught on a cloud of ice

I knocked on your door with the light in my eye
But it got stuck on the cold wood

I knocked on your door with the stillness of my
    body
Straight up like a tree
But the leaves at the tip of its branches were silent

I knocked on your door and I understood too late
That there was no one at home

And the door tied me to the deadness of its own
    frozen silence

Land-cry

I live in a land-cry with roots of fire
Buried beneath the stones of loneliness

I have slowly plowed the dreadful kelp
In a bitter season of rain
With the crab-heart's hunger to hold fast

A phantom ship I have risen to the river's surface
Toward the fulness of human tides
And I have thrown the crowd to the promises of the
    future

Tomorrow
We shall live in the secret planets
Of slow anger and the upright wisdom of dreams

I live in a land-cry upstream from hopes
Cast off on every lip
Already moored to the sunlight on glowing trawlers

And every word abolishes the hard lie
The shameful caverns of our silence

Plan For A Country (Acadie-Québec)

Behold the hour of enlightened men
With their recollection contained in the final plan
Behold the march to the future
In action growing to the rhythm of possible worlds

It is with each stroke of love, with the strength of
    dreams
That we shall climb up the hill of our fears
For the gift of a sun on everyone's skyline

It is with a pitch tuned to the space of careful words
That we shall carry back the flame of our origins
To transform our visions into lucid promises

Behold the hour of history willed
To change the misery of slaves
Into the reality of new and free men

From now on, this hour belongs to us

I Am Acadian

I curse in English every mongrel *goddamn* in the
    book
And *fuck-its* often stick in my throat
Along with *christs* flung against the *windshield*
Bleeding *medium-rare*

Had I at least a few twelve-storey *tabernacles*
And toasted *hosties*
I'd know myself to be a Québécois
Know I could blaspheme cathedrals of fear
But I am Acadian and content with aping
    Johnny-come-lately
With his shiny *Chrysler* and his picture in the papers

How much longer will it take
Before this *guy* here *runs me over*
When I *cross the street* to play with myself in a room
And they put me at last in a graveyard
Like all the others
To the tune of "You will return to dust"
And then Shit
Who says we're not that already.

I am Acadian
Which means
Stuffed dispersed bought alienated sold out
    rebellious. A here there and everywhere
Man torn open towards the future

Poem, July 1982
*Written after the death of my mother and
nephew in May
for Lise*

The day is getting greasy in the big blue frying pan
and the sun bursts like an egg yolk
in a shattering of light

When the sun has finished sweating
when it has moistened the earth by stretching out
full length on the grass and our rainbow dreams
I will pour myself a tall glass of light
and drink to your health, to your kitten-like eyes
to your breasts that you offer me for breakfast

Afterwards we will go out for a walk
to listen to the last raindrops singing
these island pools that freshen the carrots in the
        garden
and the little strawberries on the seashore at
        Anse-Bleue
that taste like love after the stormy season of
        sleepless nights
and those beer bottles that rolled under the bed
under a weeping sky with a mended heart
a ragpatch sky

One day the truth jumped up in my face and
        scratched my eyes
I saw a bird in a cage I opened the door
and the bird flew out and crashed into a window

Drops of blood stained the mattress . . .
I threw it out
my nerves were as frazzled as worn-out guitar strings
that break right when you manage to pick out the
        tune

I also threw my old song in the garbage can
for a long time afterwards I could still hear it whine

in the cold pizzas at three in the morning
the empty Mooseheads from *la Cave*
the cracked cup on the floor
the headaches, my poor head drunk with lies
the morning after a thousand and one binges
lying between the houses, on the floor, in the stairs
under the bed with cigarette burns in my navel
and my eyes in a fog

I no longer had the use of my heart
I watched my hands tremble
I listened to my belly howl

You can't *skip out* on reality

When you haven't got the cash to pay your *rent*
and your UIC doesn't come in
reality is you
it's the breakfasts you don't eat
the guts that howl loud enough to burst your
    eardrums

"Stop ruining me!
I can't stand this craziness!
Take a big bite of life!"

My words ran short of breath
and my lungs could no longer write poems

I had curtains over my eyes
and cement in my shoes

My life was a tavern
and I didn't even feel like
playing the blues on the piano.

Maybe you're surprised I'm telling you all this,
but anyway . . .

When you dream of razor blades
it's time to let go, to take a look in the mirror

to get new clothes rip up your dirty laundry move
and then
one day
let yourself be caught by surprise
by a smile wide as the sea

I used to scream, now I talk

Poets have no right to be silent
there is no shame in loving and saying I love you
you turn me on, you knock me off my feet, you
    excite me, you transform me
you make me die

Come tuck me in, caress me, make me discover boats
sailing on the clouds
make me smell the little red strawberries
like sunsets between your fingernails

Come here so I can hold you close to me
we'll go lie down on the golden sand
watch the sun go down to dip its toe in the sea
take its bath so we can find ourselves in a morning
beautiful as a gentle heart on your lips
as your breast that you offer me for breakfast

I hear the love beating its wings in your eyes
I feel myself growing younger under my greying hair
Soon I will crawl around like a little child
I will flirt we will make our loves
with little kisses all over our bodies

We'll love each other so passionately
that the room will catch on fire
and everyone on Maple Street will see
that love is truer than all the houses around Lake
    Jones
truer than *Another World*
more powerful than the Prime Minister
that guy, and the bankers, and the presidents
of big companies

They're the ones who should be thrown in the
    garbage
I shouldn't have to tighten my belt
so that my money can grease the pigs
that are already so fat they block the sun
as if the light belonged to them
as if those bandits could hook
their interest rates on the sun
just for the thrill of showing off
while ordinary people throw themselves off the pier

Once I drowned I hit bottom
but no one else will send me down to the rocks
    under the sea
I have bright eyes clear eyes the sun in my eyes
and all those who marched through the streets of
    Fredericton
all those men and women
from Baie Ste-Anne to Kouchibouguac
from Kedgwick to Chatham from Saint John to
    Caraquet
all those who demand their rights
their land their livelihood
they, too, have the sun in their eyes

And my mother my nephew did too
but the manufacturers of fear
the millionaires of despair
built brick walls twelve feet wide
and a hundred feet high to block out the light

The heart was no longer beating the body didn't
    want to follow
they went to sleep they left in the merry month of
    May
le mois de Marie le mois le plus beau quand les filles
    sont belles

   au ciel au ciel au ciel
   j'irai la voir un jour . . .

Another day later on
when I am less miserable
when I can root through her suitcase
take out the old photos
look at her blue dress without sobbing
another day later on
I shall also remember that swallow
that flew into the church at St-Anselme
and I shall sit down at my typewriter

I'll write you a long love poem Mam
I'll sing you a love song Yves

My voice will carry so far
that I won't even need a microphone
I'll shout over the screeches of tractors
the speeches of politicians
the noise of the machines of power

I'll shout at the top of my lungs:

Youth has a right to the future!
Old people have a right to happiness!
Love cannot be bought!

I still have a lot more to say
Maybe later

I've had accordions in my lungs
ever since I met you
I want to dance to the sound of fiddles from home
I want to celebrate
I want you

Come tuck me in
Come comfort me
Come touch me

The sun is setting

It is time to sleep in your arms

I love you

I love you

Poem For Lise

As when the sunlit crystals shine
On the white sea of the snow
You come to me a soft beam a dust of flame
Waking in my eyes the quick spark of a child

I play at running upon this moss of wool
That melts into sonorous dust-clouds
To fill the sky full of stars
Like in your eyes a pathway to the heart
There you are snow sunshine dance blue snow storm
In a winter cloak in a seaport
And every day you teach me to travel
As far as the dawn of snowflakes
The simple imagination of things
The red-hot spark of life

To love you is to let myself be taken
Into gentle threads of golden nets
Where the flower of time is sleeping
On warm promises of caresses bursting into bloom

As when your sunshine eyes come alight
I become that innocent season
And I love to stretch out near your warmth
You my beloved my hearth my candle
You woman fulness awakening
Rainbow and diamond
You Lise
Like the miracle of snow

With Her

With her I no longer fear myself
With her I no longer fear my own dark night
With her I have learned again to see hear touch
With her I have become a traveller

Past Midnight

Past midnight past midday
The moon and the sun live with me

I write in the certainty of day and night
I have found love again while walking at her side
And poetry at the end of my road
At the heart of life in the rhythm of outings
In my desire to tell of the miracle of being here

Past midnight past midday
The moon and the sun live with me

Time Turns To Tenderness

Time turns to tenderness my love
At the simplest touch of your gaze
With the waking of the skyline over the city's white
    dawn
Where the speech of multitudes buzzes and murmers

Time turns to tenderness my love
In the stretching of bodies the mewling of cats
And the prayers of grasshoppers
The offering to the light that plays in the curtain

Time turns to tenderness my love
When water caresses the skin
And far above the call of sirens
Sings my joy of knowing you alive

Time turns to tenderness my love
With the euphoric dance of snowflakes
The warm presence of the sun in the heart of crystals
The spontaneous movement of things that greet you

Time turns to tenderness my love
And I offer you with each breath
The secret life of the world's breathing
Where exactly
At this instant
Time turns to tenderness
My love

Birth

I am a moving aquarium
Filled with coloured fish
Blue-banded angel-fish
Crimson clowns
A grouper with brown spots
A flying-fish
A yellow sturgeon
A few Siamese suckers
Several moon-fish from Sheba
A lung-fish nursing its lungs
Here and there trout barbotte
Spotted catfish with red angle-fish
An electric eel lighting up pink sea-horses
An enormous green Muraena beside a reticulate
    dragonfly
And even a water dragon from Indonesia and
    crocodiles

I am a moving aquarium
Filled with coloured fish
And the frail window which separates me from you
Holds back my desire to return to the ocean
Mother-sea of my first birth

Extract From *The Trigram Of The*
Unfathomable Heart

I

Oracles
Wei Tsi-ting-ki Tsi

The fire dances
On an icy mirror.
It is time for sacrifice,

For giving up,
For transcendence of self.

And the flame melts
In the game

Of the universe.

HUGUETTE LÉGARÉ

A professional writer and historian, Huguette Légaré was born in Qué-
bec in 1948 and completed post-graduate studies at Laval in 1972. She
was awarded the Prix du Cercle du Livre de France in 1973 for her
novel, *La Conversation entre hommes,* and second prize in Radio-
Canada's radio drama competition in 1975.

Publications: Poetry: *Le Ciel végétal,* (La Pensée universelle, 1976),
La Tempête du pollen (Éditions Saint-Germain-des-Prés, 1978), *L'Amarinée*
(Éditions Saint-Germain-des-Prés, 1979), *Brun Marine* (Éditions d'Acadie,
1982), *Le Cheval et l'éclat* (Éditions Naaman, 1985).

Fiction: *La Conversation entre hommes* (Le Cercle du Livre de
France, 1973).

The Coffee Cup

I have put my heart in your coffee cup. Drink it. And
talk to it. Make it a beer glass that withstands the

shock of long years. Coffee comes by boat. Here there are industries and their little bells with stars, little star-bells.

I have put my heart into your beer glass. Drink it. I have put my heart into your cigarette. Smoke it. Make it a tiny fag-end of a harbour.

Put my heart into your pleasure, so that I may not be only a haven in appearance.

Here the snow is easy to look at: it is white, it is beautiful. Put my heart in your boots. Crush it a little, that's good. To be crushed a little bit is a good thing in life. The misery of love: that exists.

Sinister Ritual

The forty-year-old woman who still lives with her parents, the ones who have a big house and a heart-shaped driveway in front of the door, is getting ready to go out, like every afternoon, to walk her dog around the neighbourhood on a leash.

She speaks to the servant-girl: "I think I am going to put on my coat that does not show the dirt, my thick-soled, hardwearing shoes, the blouse that I wore yesterday, because they are rebuilding the street and dust is gathering."

Pollen-tempest

Tempest groomed from the pollen of pubescent
    dandelions
Elastic spirit of the fields' constricted strength
The pollen flies in the air, a magic pipeline
Our ox-eye daytime is being lopped off
And shoots upwards and broadens out

Thick bumblebees like the tiny paws of Spring
   puppies
Notes more rapid than the tranquility of pollen
Big black ophidian spots on the dandelions
An aerodynamic intricacy of fake stingers
Passing over pathways of still-furled ferns

The Moon

The man who did not wish to keep
Silent his wish to love and weep
Pressed my fingers soft beneath
His eyes: our lips trembled in one breath

We loved to watch our breathings' flow
My fingers stroked his loving eyes
Evening was falling, rolled in many-coloured irises
Falling on our thoughts' sea-echo

Laughing as pledged roses laugh
Under a local and short-lived moon
Allowed to build the truth at last
On a kiss given a bit too soon

The hopes of birds before me then
Are seen as a drawn-out thread when
I rethink your zeal for love's pains
That led us under raspberry canes

When the ghost of a swallow passed
Under a moon short-lived and local
The brushwood's fruits away were cast
Once more. Your smile gave the signal.

Beside The Hotel

The train comes in to the station with a sigh echoing
daisies or the sound of a pipe being emptied on a tree
The train comes in to the harbour's tip, behind the

warehouses on the quay, where the heat keeps us from thinking and makes us want to cry, heat like the kind of night when it gets dark inside the house and grey outside
On the plain decorated with sheets of sand, the sky speaks: "Yes, I am leaves, yes I am heads of hay"
Among the tiny flowers with the fins and umbels of dead herring left out in the rain, the grass is yellowed like hair when it gets grey
The sea has the simplest waves I have seen so far, spanned by piquant gleams of thistles and the glances of birds' eyes, beside the hotel with its flower beds and shaggy floors

It seems that waterside horses prefer the colour blue to other colours and that they truly know more about life from hearing the sea with its steady magnificent roar
The sails that have been lifted up to dry form funny leaf figures in the night
The sea knows what the weather is doing, what is meant by the dark sky with its stars covered in blackberries, what can come of a love which finds itself nearly too beautiful, with heartbeats too fine and the green lips of vegetation lying along the high sea, light as tiny leaves, and where there are quiet boats that mourn, love too strong, like the sea entering a house
We shall always hear love with some difficulty because the ears of the wind are full of salt

The old man speaks to his fishing boat that he has built by the old methods: "Come on, love, we are going out on the sea"

DYANE LÉGER

Dyane Léger was born in Notre-Dame-de-Kent and is a poet, photographer and painter. She won the Prix France-Acadie in 1981 for her first book of poetry, *Graines de fées,* and has published her work in *Éloizes, Estuaire* and *Cahier bleu.*

Publications: Poetry: *Graines de fées* (Éditions Perce-Neige, 1980; new editions: Éditions d'Acadie, 1985), *Sorcière de vent!* (Éditions d'Acadie, 1983).

Non-fiction: *Visages de femmes* (Éditions d'Acadie, 1987).

The Hangar Of The Haunted

There was no wind. A few trees had seen it, tail between its legs, going away yapping. There were no more colours. Black fatigue boots had crushed the colours of dayflight. There was nothing else ... nothing other than a blindfolded Ballerina pirouetting innocently in this absurd vagueness. Nothing but the sky, a Summer sky, hidden in the depth of time, in an abandoned house.

In an abandoned house at the bottom of time you sit, feet on your suitcase, a little aloof, like a statue of a cracked Immaculate Conception. You do not look at the medals of the slain soldiers who had turned halfway around the world so as to come back and be hooked on the branches of your brambles. You no longer reread your love letters that yesterday's stamps have bayoneted, beaten up. Lately ... you had even stopped entreating the sarcasm of the Christ nailed to the top of the door. You hardly dream any more.

Do you hear the bitter laughter, dripping from the perverse calendar; it flows softly, continually under the door of your room? Your cold room, with its jets of frozen orgasms hanging down from the rust, its dream-me white lies fluttering in the fangs of bat winds, its spleen of ruined love-affairs pushed against the windows? ... Ah, those sad sad windows ... do you know how to listen to the whisper of the spider webs which compose this palace woven out of boredom, the grating of the bleached and ragged old things that fidget, and the death-rattles of our young lives, yours and mine, who have imprisoned the Sybil in the Hangar of the Haunted? Listen ... listen with all your ears. The Sybil, she suffers forever the horrible deaths that age inflicts on tiny blushes. While you stand forever on the threshold, feet on your suitcase, lost in a salty daydream.

You become like a madwoman. You relive your life like a step danced against the beat. You see once more the gentle Mayfly, who plays life's trumpets until its final crescendo carries a corpse to the village. It brushes against your body, penetrating the antechamber. You watch it strangle the music, drown your scriptgirl. It goes away . . . without beating about the bush.

At the sight of its old child, the corpse stops . . . smiles. Your photo bursts out laughing! And your house collapses, like a crystal ballerina shattered under the blow of a broom.

Latent Lesbians

> Most often, most naturally, I put on rouge.
> After all, what spreads more easily than blood?
> Michaux

You loomed up from nowhere, glued yourself to my mirror like frost to a pond. You were an angel, the rough sketch of a beauty hand-drawn by a mad artist who had gone off in a gust of wind, leaving you behind in the café. You were Esther Paradise.

The first time I set eyes on you, you were the picture of classic elegance. Seated and aloof, you were drawing smoke from your cigarette. The smoke surrounded your frail shoulders like hair; your cigarettes stretched out catlike toward your feet and your fag-ends swelled the ashtrays like penises inflamed by love. Esther Paradise. You were the envy of every woman; and still today, their miserable jealousy can hardly vindicate their too-great admiration.

A ravishing huntress with a marble soul, you would weaken your prey with sweetness and with subtlety; and before they could become conscious of your ruses, you would thread them on your rapier. And your men, your men like bouquets of affection spouted happy perfumes for you, for you, Esther, who continued smoking as if nothing were going on.

You were still smoking when McGlory walked in; he did not even look at you. Stunned, you set your trap so badly you caught yourself in it! Needless to say, the consequences, your actions and words radiated from your white wedding gown like an never-ending string of movie credits. First it was the church, then the hotel, do you remember? . . .

A honeymoon poured out cascades of love that drifted like snow on the field of common sense. A throng of slaves flowered as white roses. A naked virgin provided the wedding night. Inside the nuptial chamber, Aphrodisia evoked lascivious melodies and McGlory poured the wine that you drank . . . and drank . . . and drank.

Then, you hooked your body to his and pitched through the waltz of eroticism. One and two, and one two three, and tra la la, tra la la! It was just like Christmas! Laughter leaped in the curtains like ribbons of flame! Roses exploded in crimson gaiety! Pleasure was sparkling and reality electrified the impossible. It was the 15th of August! Do you remember? . . . Everything was so exquisite . . . little love birds dancing all around!!!

Then came the intermission to the great concerto of love's magic. Your unfinished desires, Esther, returned backstage to talk, to talk among themselves . . . but the meaning of their conversation, repeated like this, for the thousandth time, lost itself on the merry-go-round of futility . . .

Calmly, a plaster-cast silence numbed the wine. And you, you sat on your bed, pale as pearly snow, and watched the recumbent figures sculpt your awkward gestures, your inconsequential words, and you thought yourself long forgotten.

You puffed on your cigarette . . . You watched your husband's belly rising and falling, falling and rising in the rhythm of a man who has got what he wanted. You detested that obscene stomach, as hairy as a monkey's, that stomach that was rising and falling. You would have preferred a corpse beside you.

— Esther! What has come over you? Have you lost your mind? Please stay in your bed! You must not break the literary sequence. What? Speak up, I can't hear you. Cigarettes! . . . You want me to go to the variety store? . . . Shit. Esther, can't you see that I'm in the middle of a poetic drama! What? . . . Of course I am the poet! Of course I must make sure that you are comfortable. Why, you are impossible! I shouldn't have made you smoke. Oh, stop complaining! Have you no sense of poetry? No mercy? You know damn well that my neuroses weep all night, that I have to stay up all night to take care of them, cradle them, coddle them! Esther, you know that I'm no longer a twenty year old! O.K., O.K., if that's the way it has to be, I'll go. Wait here. I'll be back soon.

— Oops! Now what? . . . God, I don't believe this. Who are you? What are you doing, sitting like that right in the stairway? Do you want me to break both my legs? Who are you anyway? What do you want?

— The reader? . . . Oops! . . . So sorry. Listen, things are not running smoothly for me today. I have to take myself out of this text for a few minutes. I have to go to the variety store. Esther is out of cigarettes and she can become a bitch if I cross her. You must understand, I am only the poet. I have given birth to a character;

but as you know, they're like children, they grow up to have a mind of their own, go their separate ways and often they develop caprices. Just between you and me, fictitious people are so vain, they begin to think they're real people and inherit all kinds of odd habits. Angels like my Esther marry all the sins at once! So listen, do me a favour and don't let on . . . I'll be back in a jiffy and I'll finish the text. O.K.?

Relaxed, Esther lights her cigarette . . . For a long time she watches her red cancer bringing to a halt everything outside herself. Peeping through the curtain, she notices that without the moon the sky is as empty as she is; and as she clings to the one who continues to sleep and snore as if there were nothing else, something in her is damaged forever. In this fallen state, Esther feels the extent of her solitude.

If there were to be another chapter to this story, it would surely begin here.
— Esther, if you had known how to sleep, your dreams would have turned your pain into a happy-ending fairy tale. Your perfect man, your knight errant, your prince charming would have surely filled your future with happiness. You would have gone off like a frantic horse on a gale of winged laughter! If only that night you had known how to live to the limit, galloping all the way!

A few days ago you were killing your husband. Yesterday, you were attending the funeral of your love and you did not even cry. You stayed there, rooted like a tree, a forest in asphalt. At first, I had the impression that you wanted to annoy me, then I realized that you probably did not remember a thing . . .

— Esther, do try to remember. It was late . . . Very late . . . You were in your bedroom . . . McGlory lay beside you. You were smoking. You still smoked while the blood streamed from your victim. Esther, try to remember. You are not at the movies! Good Lord,

Esther, if you have no self-respect, think of others, think of me!...of the reader! He would be disappointed by such a lousy performance. He isn't interested in reading a description of the dead man and wouldn't be impressed by a description of the flowers, tears, and prayers; he wants to experience your innermost feelings, the state of your soul! Please Esther, snap out of it!

— A murder? What do you mean, a murder? Me? But you've gone out of your mind! You are nuts! Why should I kill him, why me?

— O.K., O.K., what good is it? It's no use. You saw me; you know I killed him.

— Now the decent thing left to do is to explain why. It's because like you, Esther, I hate men. Those primitive heads that science styles in modern ways, those pale princes enthroned in beer-halls, putting the make on their Saturday night prey...You've seen them, between two sighs, devouring their victim's sex, erecting their own towers of Babel, seeding graveyards with infant carcasses?

— On the other hand, Esther, I must confess...Faced with a man's love, his caresses, his intimate promises, I quiver like a tiny maple leaf. "You are so beautiful, I die in your eyes. Your legs cling to my heart. I love you." He loves me and there it is. I have become his *pièce de résistance*, his wedding cake iced with royal jelly, wild strawberries, and cashew nuts.

— Oh! to eat of this cake that has the taste of your laughter and your smiles...What I want is a hand as gentle as a gust of rose-winds, a hand gentle with love, a touch so light yet alive with such a passion that it would drive me wild! A mouth, lips, your lips, embracing mine softly, so softly that I would turn over in feminine delight and become a perfumed wind of tender poetry.

— Esther? Did you say something? . . . Oh, don't play dead. When I spoke to you, I watched you out of the corner of my eye. Although the stiffness of your character was able to disguise your feelings, the gleam in your eyes betrayed you. I saw your eyes light up like giant Christmas trees and your flesh begin to quiver to strange and forbidden rhythms. Stop pretending that nothing is happening. We both know that . . .

— Esther, for God's sake what are you doing? . . . You have no right! I forbid you! Esther, you must not make McGlory rise out of your beautiful eyes. He is dead. I killed him. Esther, I like you a lot, I would let you do whatever you want, I shall do everything you ask; but I beg you, do not bring McGlory back to life. No one will understand. No one will believe it! We shall be ruined. Can you imagine? Is that what you want? . . .

— Esther, I beg you. Do not let your little-girl caprices destroy everything we have. Do not bury the rest of our lives in a shroud of silence. Listen, Esther, if you want, I can make you beautiful and young forever. You know I can . . . You will live in a villa on the edge of a sunlit island like you always dreamed. You will wear dresses of pearl, emerald, and jasmine. You will have everything your heart desires. You will be adored, fulfilled! You know that I can do all that! You know that for you, Esther, I will do anything at all. But in order to do that, you must tell me, only me, only me in a whisper, that McGlory is dead. Tell me that while I was panic-stricken and searching for a direct object and while the storm hummed with the snow-clad laughs of spiders, that you, Esther, for your own amusement, you threw confetti of madness into my coffee and that I am hallucinating!!! Tell me, tell me anything, I want only to believe you . . .

HENRI-DOMINIQUE PARATTE

Born in Berne, Switzerland in 1950, Henri-Dominique Paratte now lives in the Annapolis Valley and teaches at Acadia University. He is also a professional translator, a consultant in cultural policy and the literary editor of Les Éditions du Grand Pré.

Publications: Poetry: *Virgée Tantra Non Arpadar* (Éditions Grassin, 1972), *La Mer écartelée* (Éditions Naaman, 1978), *Dis-moi la nuit* (Éditions d'Acadie, 1982).

Translations: *Cheval des Îles* (Ragweed Press, 1984), *Poésie acadienne contemporaine/Acadian Poetry Now* (Éditions Perce-Neige, 1985), *Anne: la maison aux pignons verts* (Ragweed Press, 1985; also with Éditions Québec/Amérique, Presses-Pocket, etc.), *Langues et littératures au Nouveau-Brunswick* (associate editor; Éditions d'Acadie, 1985).

Blood Red
> *in memory of Gatien Lapointe*

Through the eyelids
The sun sprays
Red madder
Flowers of blood in the depths of the head
I no longer know
Where is outside
Where is inside
Only this flower only this blood
Through the eyelids
I exist and no one in the world gives a damn
I exist and I don't give a damn about the world
I
You
She
I no longer have an age nor a sex
Only one enormous vein
In the throbbing sunlight

In a com-pu-ter-ized world
Computers everywhere computers that track down
        computers that
Capture everything

The computer-vampire will drink
Neither my sunlight
Nor my blood
Red like Brazilian butterflies
Under phosphorescent
Eyelids.

* * *

I am the tropical dance floor of naked Indian dancers
Amazon head-hunters
I hunt for texts
In the great jungle of the imaginary
I no longer know
Where is outside
Where is inside
I don't give a damn
Butterfly-texts beat at my waist
Like so many countries
My belly a universe
Acadians can be found as far off as the Falklands
Indians of the western world
Red Acadie

Eyes closed
Red blood red sunlight red Acadie
Red fishermen who break the windows
Of government offices
Red tears on the bodies
Of dead men in the sea anonymous phantoms
Red pig's blood on the sleeping earth
Red scar of Grand-Pré beaches
Évangéline Beach
Red Glooscap
Summer sunlights of early mornings in Marseilles
Sunlight of Corsican wines
like veins where bursts from despair
A dawning of liberty

RED
RED

RED
RED

Red
of my revolutions which have not taken place
    nor perhaps ever will take place
Red of my revolutions betrayed hunted down in
which I no longer believe
while hoping that others
believe in them
striking while the iron of dreams is red hot
Red of the *RCMP*
on Canadian fifty-dollar bills
that at any rate are not worth
any more than the paper
they are written on

Blood red something that comes from the distance
my verses written in red ink
the glass of red wine that I drink
to the health of Acadie
In a last reflection
Red incarnate

Red for dying
never

I Read Poetry...

I read poetry in the lines of your hand, in the lace of
your sex, in the sweet fruit of your breasts, in the foam
on the rising tide, in the glitter of ice still present in
May in front of the Acadian pioneer village in the
Évangéline area.
I read poetry beyond words, in the wind from
Évangéline Beach that comes to whip our faces when
our steps are marked in the sand, the memories of
Chateaubriand on the coasts of Brittany, I read poetry
which belongs to no one, no more to us than to others,
poetry which leaks, like sand through our fingers, like

light through our eyes, like the sweetness flowing through our mad kisses. I read poetry in the warmth of the world when the apple trees in the valley are in the midst of bursting into enormous snow-flowers.

ROBERT PICHETTE

Born in 1936 in Edmundston, Robert Pichette has worked as a journalist, a television producer and a civil servant. He is currently employed with the Atlantic Canada Opportunities Agency. A fellow of the Royal Society of Arts of Great Britain, he has written a number of studies on historical subjects and heraldry.

Publications: *Chimères, poèmes d'amour et d'eau claire* (Éditions d'Acadie, 1982), *Bellérophon* (Éditions d'Acadie, 1987).

Miscou
Et in Arcadia ego.

Where have the blue herons gone that I loved so much, standing still near the reeds rustling in the dead waters of the marsh, only two strides from the sea, broad, becalmed, and indifferent?

Away! We must leave.

Already the sand is no longer warm on the deserted beach where your footsteps used to crush the purplish seaweed.

Away! We must leave.

An illusion has died. This Summer is no longer ours and this desolate beach denies me the memory of our love. I can no longer find periwinkles, nor the old discarded basket, nor the messageless bottle come from who knows where stranded by chance on Miscou, the lovely, calm, peaceful, placid accomplice to our love.

Away! We must leave.
The old mottled blanket no longer retains your shape
and the pitiless tide, with its monotonous regularity,
has long since erased any memories of our joy. The
lighthouse, witness to our happiness, becomes threat-
ening, and these inquisitive but prudent gulls are no
longer our friends.

Farewell, Miscou! Good-bye, my soul!

Imaginings

Across a garnet-red velvet sky
strange birds flew
whose names we did not know
come from we know not where
going god knows where
geographers of uncharted skies,
tightrope walkers, acrobats,
light and ridiculous objects of the wind.

Ancient Tapestry

> "*There are far fewer ungrateful persons than one
> believes; for there are certainly fewer generous people
> than one thinks.*"
>
> Saint Evremond

Still I have a taste for you
like that for a finely woven tapestry
pricked out with a thousand flowers
embroidered with patience
for a forgotten Crusader.

Still I have a taste for you
for your legs like a nervous fawn
for your eyes large as lakes
where dreams grow dark

for your fine eyelashes
for the curved line of your loins.

Still I have a taste for you
for the even beat of your heart
for the taut points of your breasts
for your white hips
doe in repose
breathless with love.

Still I have a taste for you
for your faint smile
as you sleep
for your tapered fingers
not even holding the shadows
nor even less so my love
nor running water
no more than your lies.

Still I have a taste for you
for your swan's neck
for your anxieties
quickly calmed
for your almost false prudery
for your rest
in the crook of my arm
for your partly opened lips
for your unfinished dreams.

Still I have a taste for you
. . . Alas!

MARTIN PITRE

Born in 1963 in Robertville, New Brunswick, Martin Pitre studied
Communications in Moncton and Paris and presently works as a
journalist with *Acadie Nouvelle.*
  His writing has been published in *Éloizes* and in the anthology

Poésie acadienne contemporaine/Acadian Poetry Now (Éditions Perce-Neige, 1985).

Publications: *À s'en mordre les dents* (Éditions Perce-Neige, 1982).

Dark And Light

the dishes are piling up. i am afraid that an avalanche of faïence might sweep me even farther down in this gloomy basement space. a *pitre* is a clown who is only a king in his caracol. he has only one moment of grace to make his little bells laugh.

i put my eyes in your head, and blinded you. a funny detour for feet that wanted to lead you in their step . . . but at your smile, my head dims, the lights become dumb, and there is only room for your joy alone, which becomes mine. near the trees, childhood is crying out its future as it rolls in the grass. and turning, turning around in a ring of hopes and fatalities. and i am happy. and my lips are grinning. and my arms are holding me back. and my mouth is biting into my soul.

and i am happy, so happy that i want to kill myself in order to brand this odious joy with the stigma of eternity. i want my will to be done. and i am god! and my megalomania strangles me with my own arms, amorous tentacles. and my story lays me beneath your breasts so that your weight is for me a breastplate and shield against everything outside me.

dark and light. my story unravels the moments that it has not assimilated. and i would like to dance. to dance, beating my head against the melody of a rigadoon spread out on a still dirty platter, always dirty, soiled eternally! until i decide otherwise.

However, there is no way to do it. as long as this basement has not made the effort to become an upper storey, never will the trash be taken out. as long as

there is a page to wrap up a dream, my own, actually
i impose it on you: my eyes will not fall anywhere else
but on your head caressed by this crazy fan of hair.

A Wrinkled Rough Copy

a blank page. history of travels at war with the known.
discovering the unknown through the spirals of your
ideas. your ideas, like a family of lice eating up your
skull. having so much empty space in the eyes and
putting in it nothing but silence . . . and telling you
again of the times for kissing *à la française*, cheeks
joined by disintegrated distance.

we had written a few delightful trifles on a wall-page.
we hear them, sometimes, when the breath of your
perfume sweetens the trees. forest. womb of life. the
floating sense of life-giving ecstasy. you are born from
a root, and you twist, stretch, slap yesterday's face,
while licking the fingers of the future.

an empty dirty-white page. incompletely erased.
smudges of dumbfounded glimpses. the return, after
such a longing, should have been, from arm to hand, an
expanding force. a long wished-for return, experienced
like a desired birth. the utmost suffering never to be
equaled.

a page. a rough copy wrinkled by too many failures.
too many wrong moves. the boat, disabled, lies in front
of your footsteps like a carpet of beautiful memories
for the times to come.

let us sleep.

it was the moment to say: I will love you.

In Fact . . .

1.
In fact, you see, all of us are
a little bit lost in the thrust of our
bodies toward the incommensurable emptiness
of another's eyes.
Then why should we have only a
single compass that points to the same north
when we are all looking for
something different.
And if your gaze carries farther than
mine, don't you believe that you should
distinguish the ocean's tear in order at last
to dredge me up from the deep.
Basically, all of this to tell you that it
would be useless to look for me where I
think you are.

2.
I am frustrated, I know it.
No need to remind me of it.
I am in the imperative present and too young to be
twenty in my American wants.
And I am a wound that you go over like a fingernail
grating on skin.
And I press you too hard, a poultice, but you tell me
I ought to peel you off.
But slowly, you say.
I am not obliging, but useful.
No, I want to pull you off with a sharp yank.
That hurts, too, but not for so long a time.
And then, who knows?
Maybe when you've been pulled off, the pus of my
wound will go away with you.

3.
Because, once again, you see, when the door closed
you came back to me.

I did not see you because the blade of my razor was
gleaming in the break of your absence.
And, tasting this blood which, already, was making me
come alive, I dripped, little by little, on the light-ray
that cut through the landing and maintained the
scattered shadow of your returnings.

MAURICE RAYMOND

Born in Campbellton, New Brunswick, in 1954, Maurice Raymond
studied at universities in Moncton and Rimouski, and now works as a
baker. His poems have been published in *Éloizes* and other literary
journals.

Publications: *Implorable désert* (Éditions d'Acadie, 1988).

The Evidence And The Miracle

if a gardener is digging
it's because there is soil

if a fountain is lighting up
its gardens of fresh water
it's because the sea exists
and if in heaven
angels are passing by in tears
it's because so many things are impossible

Simply To Believe . . .

simply to believe
that silence
is the fire's mouth
and that love
is the mirror
of the pacified sea

simply to believe

that this kiss
lost among shadows
is an unceasing source
of light and blood

to believe simply
that a poem
is a foundation
that each word
is a stone
that this wall
is transparent

to believe
simply
that a poem
is a foundation

The Limits Of Speech

your faces without light
in the darkening of my heart

your chalk-mark of absence
on the felt of my blood
all that a song emprisons
from the wings of the sea
to the bites of death

Unstable Passers-by

lovers ruined
flowing in bouquets
under a tiny wicker bridge

stretched sunshine
whose webs burst
one by one
as tears do

a small wasted dream
with the face of a flower . . .

Builders Of The Void

on the crest of the abyss
there where light copies itself
we are weaving glass cages
which with one breath
   when darkness comes
will crumble into our destinies

The Wind

that light on the soil among piled-up shadows
and dust

that little square of blind light
on the quay

it is cold
the wind only
forming pitiful shapes

and my gaze
that is lost in the night

my gaze only
blind and miserable
forming and reforming shapes in the night

RINO MORIN ROSSIGNOL

Rino Morin Rossignol has worked as a professional writer, translator and journalist. He worked for the Government of New Brunswick and was the editor of *Le Matin* during its existence. He now lives in Montréal.

Publications: Poetry: *Les Boas ne touchent pas aux lettres d'amour* (Éditions Perce-Neige, 1988).

Theatre: *Le Pique-nique* (Éditions Perce-Neige, 1982).

Essays: *Rumeur publique* (critical edition with Anne-Marie Robichaud, Éditions d'Acadie, forthcoming).

It Was Love ...

it was love to be sure
and I needed wings
to fly as far as your image
hovering high in my head
like a rebellious kite
escaped from the clutches of a mischievous child

it was love to be sure
and I needed wings
to struggle against this savage wind
that carried me away every time
that you came killing a kiss
on my incredulous brow

it was love to be sure
and I needed wings to love you
but I had already scattered my feathers
to the ephemeral winds of need

Baobab

The desert offers itself to me. A desert noticed from afar, suddenly surrounding me. A false desert. A desert of African outskirts. A baobab. Baobabs kill themselves trying to grow there. Twisted. Cracks everywhere. Boas hide in them. While waiting for an uncertain prey. Possibly. Your body is distant. Your body is so far away. You are buried in a baobab in the expectation of a probable pleasure. Your sex, fat as a boa, is coiled around my fantasies. My head is open to the desert. My head is full of sand. My head is the

hourglass of our adventure. Adventure wears itself out.
I would buy all the baobabs in the world to find you
again. To shake your dead branches. I have only a few
wretched words left for you. Hardly any.

III

y again Take care. Every word
a kiss for you. (Since it is i
no French kiss.) (I hope this
u are so cute when you smile.)
whole world was like you, I'd b
the whole world. Thank God,
que
ye! Bye! Au revoir. À bientôt,
ime et je t'embrasse.

not resist squeezing a
ch words in. (For my
when I'm famous.)
(Octave whistles hi

❊

A harmless fragment for a harmless story. You no
longer exist. Hardly a grain of sand in the desert. In
my head. Africa in its entirety haunts me in this dry
time. A continent on fire. My throat on fire. I am a
dragon. A dragon without malice. And you no longer
hunt dragons.

Yesterday evening you were not at home. I know it,
I telephoned. Eight rings loud and clear. As if I had
gongs in my ears. I listened to the ringing. I was here,
my eyes were there, in Boston. Gongs in my eardrums.
So I forced my most beautiful pen to write you a
magnificent letter. Too much. When you are not there,
why must I write to you? My pen flows out of itself
for you. Then I sealed the envelope quickly, afraid of
changing my mind, and I went to throw it into the

mail box on the corner of the street. I was in that envelope. Sealed up. As in a shell. I mailed myself away to join you again. Too much. The letter box wasn't at the meeting-place.

*

I always understand slowly. You have told me so over and over a thousand times. But yesterday evening the sign presented itself to me. Brutal. Immediate. No box. No letters. No *faux pas*.

This evening I am fingering the last fragment of that wingless flight. A rendez-vous that never occured. I must not telephone you any more. You are no longer there. I must not write you anymore. The mail box is no longer there. In Africa, I would have been able to slip the letter into a crack in a baobab. Boas do not touch love letters. I could have been in the envelope. Inside the baobab. Protected from the boa and *en route* to you. Why didn't I become a missionary? Or a mercenary? Or a boa-hunter? When I was twelve years old I wanted to be a martyr. I missed my vocation.

I am going downtown. To the movies. Out of sheer habit. From my head to the screen, everything is only cinema.

*

The city looms up thickly. A skyscraper scratches the itch of truth. The city looms up thickly. We scurry like crabs among its hairs. We suck up blood from the city. The city sucks up our nature. The city is grey. The sky is grey. Grey houses on grey streets. Grey sidewalks and grey pigeons. Those that no longer travel. Those that no longer have dreams. Soon we shall all be like pigeons. Picking up grains of courage on grey pavement. I have a grey complexion. Everything is grey when your ghost is walking around.

We were so fine when we were mad with love! Do you remember? One day I shall fall in love with you again and I shall paint the horizon with mad colours. The pigeons will take flight and we shall take part in their migration. Maybe. But I shall leave the city. I shall go live in a baobab. And I shall raise boas.

ALBERT ROY

A secondary school teacher in Edmundston, Albert Roy was born in Kedgwick, New Brunswick, in 1948 and received his M.A. from the Université de Moncton. He has been awarded several prizes for his writing.

Publications: Poetry: *Poèmes venteux* (Musée des Sept-Iles, 1979), *Fouillis d'un brayon* (Éditions d'Acadie, 1980), *La Couleur des mots* (published by the Commission Scolaire Fermont, n.d.), *Des Brayonneries, poèmes et nouvelles* (Le Madawaska, 1985).

Fiction: *Comme à la vraie cachette* (Éditions Marévie, 1990).

Rage

asphalt unrolled
its cursed meanderings
under my childhood's feet
soiled by the breath of your souls

my forest vomited
the refuse of your towns
they prostituted my muse
for the colour of your kisses

    my barn has become
    a coffin
    my song a tombstone

my stream has drawn back
its tender branches

to the living springs
of your perverse eyes

my mother has knit
the vest of my life
and on the thorns of the years
I have made holes in it

   the piano has enclosed
   its worn-out notes in
   the cry of a voice
   made harsh by smoke

legions legions

   of bees and ants
   put yourselves in marching order
   under the banner of health

sound your horns

   and your trumpets
   and silence will ring
   the death knell of ill-starred
   hours hanging from
   the seeds of my garden

Carving

  i shall make
a carving
  that will sing
  the drive
  of tall pines
  down the Saint John

  i shall put new life into
a carving
  which will be

        like the warm breath
        of our forges
        re-lit through the
        vitality of
        our grandfathers
a carving
        which will dam up
        the legends drawn
        from our river bed
a carving
        which will speak
        for the love of wind
        for the love of earth
i shall discover
a chisel
        which will dig out
        the furrows
        where dreams deposit
        the seeds of
        a world
        of equality

Marthe la "Waitresse"

welcome
    sister the rain
    you cool down
    my dark ideas

and the silky grass
    of my yard takes advantage of this
    to say sweet nothings
    to alert crickets

and the leaves of my trees
    rustling
    have called to mind evenings
    when we vowed
    to each other
    eternal hopes

and I saw
  Marthe la "waitresse"
  with her tray
  of smiles
  and her eyes
  rich with dreams

  Marthe la "waitresse"
who has remained
like a comforting
kind feeling in the
heart of the mechanization
of kisses

  Marthe la "waitresse"
who has remained
like a good lighthouse
guiding my steps
toward the rivers
of life

  Marthe la "waitresse"
whom the birds
    still sing of
while copying
    the love-notes
that the wind
    transports

Marthe la "waitresse"
  whom ghosts
  call for
  repeating

    . . . two beers at the back

    one wine over there

    two bottles of sack

    to be opened with care.

ROSEANN RUNTE

Roseann Runte was born in Kingston, New York in 1948 and did her graduate work at the University of Kansas. Previously the president of Université Sainte-Anne in Church Point, N.S., Roseann Runte is now the principal of Glendon College of York University. She was awarded the Prix François-Coppée from the Académie française for her second volume of poetry, *Faux-soleils*, in 1984. She has written articles and edited books on a wide range of subjects.

   Publications: *Brumes bleue*s (Éditions Naaman, 1982), *Faux-soleils* (Éditions Naaman, 1984).

Chillote Song

Let me sing for you the Pintoya's refrain
Alluring siren of the reefs of the isle of Chiloé
Let me hum for you the dance of the scarves
That proud expression of Castillian soul in Indian
      rhythms
Let me caress you like the gentle sea-breeze
That cradles the coast and makes the lone spruce
      whisper
Let me paint for you that lace-work with which
The Pacific clothes those black spits of volcanic rock
Let me introduce you to the temple of a glacier
That breathes the pure stillness of four thousand
      years
Let me tell you the mythology of a land
Peopled with magic beings and dreamers so eloquent
That we could spend a year
That we could spend a lifetime
Without discovering the boundaries
As much earthly as imaginary
Of an island of dream and hope.

Easter Island

On an island where myth and sea mingle
In three centuries of red dust where rest

The heads of collosses beaten by the enemy
Of this people of gods or by the enemy of this
    people's gods
The secrets are silent, will not be uttered or were
    silenced.

Without eyes but not without sight, these statues
    slant
Toward the human past, toward the earth's navel;
Suspended in their march toward a known destiny
Between mountain and sea or between sky and altar
These images of the living, these lifeless corpses rest.

Irrevocably sad, broken and voiceless,
Sculptures without Pygmalion, art without creator,
Giants from an epoch without history, legends
    without souls,
Corpses without sepulchres, the wind clothes you
    with soil
And your tattooed back will grow flowers.

So kingdoms end, so disappear
The vain exploits of men, the frail dreams of poets.
From dust to rot, from rock to salt;
Sorrow's tears poured on a field of sand
Water bouquets covering their cracks, our wrinkles.

From Pubnico To Sainte-Anne-du-Ruisseau

Clouds of ebony
Let their sombre gaze wander
On these alabaster waters

Midnight sounds.
The lake breathes,
And the white vapours
Of its frosty breath
Are lost in the enormity
of the hour.

You move through life,
I follow you through
One night's landscape.

Dawn arrives.
Before us the road
Unfolds
Grey

Far

Far and grey

ROMÉO SAVOIE

Before becoming a full-time poet and painter, Roméo Savoie was, for many years, an architect. He was born in 1927 and received a Bachelor's degree, with distinction, from École des Beaux-Arts in Montréal. He has travelled extensively in Europe, and his paintings have been exhibited in many places including Paris, New York and Miami.

Publications*: Duo de démesure* (Éditions d'Acadie, 1981), *Trajets dispersés* (Éditions d'Acadie, 1989).

Peeping Eurydice

For Eurydice's darkness, dreamless and
Transparent, until nightfall,
Eurydice or her twin companion
From the earth to the bitter passageway
Blonde and capricious, drunk and betrothed
Her body floats, indecently arched
    I swear to you
    My hand trembles
    I walk faithfully through the labyrinth
    From the betrothed to the sweet-smelling essences.

She disappears
The shadow of a dune leads out its brood from stone

Into stone, from seaweed into water, the stillness
  takes on
The amplitude of a treacherous spirit

One might perhaps imagine her
Eurydice in the spray where
Drunkenness could be an excuse
Or an escape, an excuse
For believing, for understanding
Her willowy and
Energetic passage or
The odour of sweat or
The hint of her caress or
Her gait, her passing, her passing
Something else which would not be
An ordinary thing with an ordinary
Taste

She will not pass
Eurydice, into limbo, to the tomb
Eurydice, the merchant
Traveling
  "mad-woman
  you are trafficking with the falling day
  you are conniving with the fate
  that you fling out pell-mell
  to measure, to see
  to trick the vigilant
  for great is your frailty
  and seasonal is your mood."

— "Are you screaming?
Do you cry sometimes?
I would love to hear you tell me so
I would love to hear it from your mouth."

Peeping Eurydice
Each gesture posed with precision
With the precision of submissive flesh
Against denial, against the will, your own
Wickedly tamed, tamer

And the dog that rages
And the dog that howls
Without understanding, at the moon
Pierrot, blasted Pierrot
And your candle, Pierrot, and your door Pierrot!
   — I have no more fire-light
   The fire extinguisher has gone by
   Well before the revolution
   Well before we understood.

The second flight Eurydice, the second flight!

Sage and sombre casting spells and telling lies,
A cry of distress together with a wheedling glance
A taste for destruction, at the same time a taste for
   construction
In her fingers sand is flowing
In her fingers blood is flowing
In her fingers there is power over life and death.

"Eurydice, did you know?
In your swaying hips
  In your bobbing bottom
  In your fluid and fiery bottom
When you were looking, when you were
   looking at me?"

I said nothing.

The cloudy envelope of contradiction
Pell-mell with desire and doubt
Pell-mell with longing and rage
Pell-mell with longing to fly or else
To stay

My country resembles you.

I have broken remembrance and frail endurance
When you play with my body it is my head that
   bursts

When you play with your body it is my body that
   dies
Neither tolerance, nor the will for relief nor the
   capacity to assume
I am whining out of deception and bitterness.

"You have the body of a water hen
An unsubdued fondness
Two reserves flowing with the caprices
   of short-lived and equivocal showers
Two short-lived and equivocal directions
Two orientations
Two opposed poles."

Eurydice in her stride of darkness
Over the setting sunlight
Over suitability and order
Overboard
Heritage engraved but not to be remade
But not to be learned
Heritage an insolence, the insolence of pride, the
   insolence of knowing the insolence of no longer
   asking or begging
A faithful and unfaithful proud daughter.

At night Eurydice
No daylight too strong to permit you
Or flight too cowardly to tell you
When you are reborn from your ashes
When the flame is dead and buried
When from your hillock you understand
The frightful distress of the unconquered
The frightful isolation of your lack of submission
Your death like your life
Will not make sense — no sense.

In our unravelled and tormented memories
In our wild memories
In our memories which juggle with familiarity
   with the despair of living
   or the desire to forget

EURYDICE YOUR DEATH EURYDICE

I do not want to think of it
I have been cast off to wander
I am the mad and spirited troubadour
I am the buried kite that moves under the weight of
    the earth
I wander and I shake off my responsibility to make
    assurances
I shake off the weight you place upon me
Eurydice for her cradle, her coffin.

Eurydice, my Eurydice, flouted, deceived

With stars, with the sheet of water which covers,
    right to the tip
Of your snow-covered feet.

I have in my pride
    imagined otherwise
Do you want to hear my story
Do you want me to speak to you
I, the survivor of Eurydice?

No one knows the emptiness
The burden of the emptiness
A shell heavier than a weight
One used to wandering
The bestial refrain that recalls
The resonance of the bestial refrain
Neither glimmers among shadows
Neither reflections nor difference
Pell-mell the lukewarm half-heartedness, the grey
The heavy grey of indifference
The grey weight of the grisaille.

I have forgotten the rest
I want to forget now
I want to forget you, Eurydice
I want to think of you no longer
Neither to imagine you, nor to contemplate

what might have been another
Eurydice
from somewhere else in another time.

The Idea Of Leaving

arriving here in this place
making sure that everything is ready
asking unending questions
imagining no matter what
allowing myself to be stoned by confusion
having certainties
breaking time's censure

I want to tell you the story of my life
or my death

you have passed through the corner of the shadow
of a single footstep
the canoe overturned on the lawn
the charcoal from an old fire
a few objects like bugaboos
our laughs
and other boats hoisting their sails
the idea of running away
while leaving traces of our passage
summer flows through your arms
the sea is greeting the furious gallops
of those traces that we leave behind

the sea is calm this morning
you moved close to the light
and time broke in two

death has left behind it all
the questions raised by others   we are
bruised by the cycles of our traditions
the crime is hidden behind the mirror
we must not look into it

I have approached silence in a different way
the ordinary is an animal that lashes out
when it is no longer coddled
throwing myself against the beast
watching the intersection of shadows
in a copse of shrubs   contemplating the incessant
    rhythm
of the wave   understanding something
that could come from somewhere else
the non-sense   the unequal relations

The Crowd

The crowd grimaces and gesticulates
it is a roisterer   its animal movement
scrawls abstract stigmata
in the light of strident reflections
our bodies draw near each other   intermingle
we are dissolved inside the crowd
penetrated   lynched   drunk up

we have also said
a body is frail
having known it we should have let our tears flow
rape hurts
it hardens the gaze
every thing is imaginary   almost
you take my arm in your two hands
you squeeze yourself very hard so you won't be
    afraid
as for me, I pretend

I am behind a mirror
and I watch with precaution
evaluating the unknown from a distance
going around it

INDEX

This index includes original French titles (in italics) with a page reference to the English translation. Titles of the English translations appear in roman type with the appropriate page reference.